Homemade Social Justice

Homemade Social Justice

TEACHING PEACE
AND JUSTICE IN THE HOME

Michael True

Mystic, Connecticut

ISBN 0-89622-202-0
(formerly ISBN 0-8190-0648-3 by Fides/Claretian)

Cover Design: Glenn Heinlein

First printing: July 1982
Second printing: July 1983

FOR
MARY PATRICIA DELANEY TRUE

Contents

Foreword

Michael True has undertaken a unique task. In this book
he addresses the question of how parents can pass on their
peace and justice values to their children. There have been
hundreds of books on parenting and almost as many on
raising good Christian children, but never has there been
one quite like this before. This book, for instance, takes
seriously parental interactions with teenagers. Few writers
on the family give enough attention to the mutual life of
parents with their young adult sons and daughters. Children today do not marry and settle down at a young age,
and the parenting process (and parental economic support)
can last well into a young person's late 20s, or even 30s.
Parents who expected an empty nest can find themselves
still coping with grown children who are struggling to enter
adulthood in a troubled and economically depressed time.
Michael True has six children ranging in age from 15 to 22,
and he knows from experience that the old books never
prepared this generation of parents for the challenges they
face in family life.

Nor, for that matter, has there ever before been a genera-
tion of Christian parents who espouse the particular set of
values found in Michael True, his wife, and many other
American Catholics. Their Christian commitment to prayer,
Scripture, and a sacramental communal life is manifested
in an active political concern for social justice and peace.
Private piety and political action are not separated; Catholic
Christians are now supporting, as Christians, causes that

have heretofore been seen as left-wing, liberal, or even socialist. Thus the peace and justice values that True and others are advocating include feminism, civil rights, economic justice, and the peace movement, especially anti-nuclear concerns. The visible prophets of American Catholic synthesis are, of course, people like Dorothy Day, Thomas Merton, and Daniel and Phillip Berrigan; but there is an increasing population of others out there. Faced with a nuclear threat, even the official stance of the American Catholic bishops is moving in this new direction. Surely these values are as old as the Gospels, but the present leavening of the American Catholic Church is new.

So how do Christian families do a totally new thing that has never been done before? The church has a great deal of traditional wisdom and experience in initiating individuals into Christian worship; it knows how to respond to predictable life events of birth, marriage, sin, illness, and death. Religious orders, for their part, have had hundreds of years of experience in creating celibate adult communities dedicated to evangelization and prophetic mission. But who knows how to raise children who can resist war, fight injustice, and work for the goals set out in the church's social teachings? Isn't there a problem in raising children to be simultaneously good members of their society and radical critics campaigning for change. It seems incredibly difficult for a family to manage to do so many of the old things necessary for childrearing along with the new. Especially when there is a large family, little money, and a decided lack of support from cultural institutions such as the parish, the neighborhood, the school, the government, or the media.

Michael True would be the first person to agree that the undertaking is not an easy one. He honestly faces all the inevitable failures and difficulties involved. Yes, you face criticism and hostility from others. Yes, your children rebel and turn a deaf ear. As parents you will constantly compromise and face outright failures of will and love. The enduring struggle for survival with limited resources can be draining and depressing. But the effort is more than worthwhile. Joyful surprises are also in store, for sometimes children display a parent's most cherished ideals. And the other like-minded persons you encounter working for peace and justice are an inspiration. As True says, "the company one keeps provides a life-saving support system." Indeed, there has to be élan and happiness in life and work for "no community of adults and children will form around a movement for social change that is half in love with death." Wise words indeed.

More wisdom informs the practical suggestions True gives for encouraging peace and justice in family life. Since every family faces internal and external conflicts and tensions, how they are resolved will serve as powerful lessons in peacemaking. Every family also faces questions of the just allocation of praise, blame, goods, services, and time. Justice too begins at home. Who can advocate social justice outside if family members inside are not treated fairly or given respect regardless of sex or size. Much can be done by overtly discussing and bringing into consciousness the values that are already present and operating in everyday family life. A parent can use everything that happens as an opportunity for the family to grow and learn together. In addition to responding to what turns up, parents have to actively create happenings, encounters, and communities within which their children will see modeled their parents' values. No family can do it alone. Happily, True gives a list of organizations and publications that can help a family find the necessary networks of support. In fact, this book all by itself exemplifies the support persons can give one another; it is filled with pertinent and inspiring quotes from the great, as well as actual incidents and helpful personal experiences of ordinary people. Not everyone can so nicely stress the need for hope while actually inspiring hope.

The psychological insight displayed in this book is of a very high quality. Every process of behavioral change and influence is presented intuitively, with all the proper cautions. The rewards of attention and praise are discussed along with the need to avoid punishment and guilt. The use of models is stressed, even the subtle strategy of having younger adult friends around who will seem more attractive and accessible to children than their older parents. But the importance of parents as the primary models for identification and internalization is given its true significance. Moreover, once you recognize that children and parents are in a family system together, you can understand that you start changing the system by changing yourself. Actions, as usual, always carry far more weight than words. Yet there is a healthy respect for the individual conscience and individual differences. Not everyone is called upon or is capable of the same witness; no one should be allowed to rush into draft resistance or tax resistance or other costly actions without self-awareness and reflection. Children, like everyone else, must find their own way.

But parents are there to pass on the past, as one generation has always done for another. Parents dedicated to peace and justice have a special history to convey. They have to speak of the often ignored heroes and heroines of peace, the many victories of nonviolence, the ever-renewed threats to justice and truth. A "People's History" that is not yet in books has to be recounted by those who care enough to remember the very best—and worst. Basically, peace and justice come from those who can remember and notice those things which are usually obscured. Violence and oppression can be so embedded and hidden in a social system that a special education of the eye and heart is needed for proper perception and perspective. Families are where we learn to see and feel. Only our life together produces the possibility of peace and justice, so we can start here, and now. With hope.

SIDNEY CALLAHAN

Introduction

This is a book about peace and justice values and the ways in which they are passed along, in the family, from one generation to another. Although it is based upon certain assumptions about what life is for and how life should be lived, it attempts to uphold those values without ignoring the complexities of the issues they raise or of the American society in which they are to be maintained.

Almost anyone has a nerve writing such a book. And rereading any page, I laugh to myself recalling how frequently I failed in applying a particular method, raising a particular issue, or following my own advice with one of our children.

In beginning as well as in completing this book, I kept remembering the night when, in frustration and anger, I pushed my young son out the door and onto the front porch, in 10-degree weather, after he complained for the hundredth time about our old car, our used furniture, and my doing draft counseling without pay. "Why don't you get a job that pays more money," he shouted, "so we can live like everybody else in the neighborhood?" My only response to that legitimate, even insightful question was a violent one, obviously *not* the method of teaching social justice recommended here.

One of the many difficult things about teaching social justice in a family is that each child responds differently at any given moment, so parents seldom know what the reaction or consequences will be. In time, however, some

1

things do get said and understood, almost in spite of parents themselves, particularly as they find ways of speaking and acting that enable children to make choices within a range of possibilities.

I am reminded of a friend of mine, a religious education teacher in our local parish, who recently asked a young man in a Confirmation class to read a section from the Gospel during Sunday Mass. In rehearsal, the student read a passage filled with sexist language, referring repeatedly to "man," "him," "mankind." When my friend suggested that perhaps the reader could substitute "person," "him or her," or "people," the student said, "I'm not sure it makes much difference whether I say 'man' or 'person.'"

"Well, that's all right, Brian," the teacher continued. "Why don't we just leave it for now and let you make the choice on Sunday as to which version is better." On Sunday, the young man read "people" and "him or her," instead of the sexist terms, thus taking one small step for personhood in that particular parish.

That non-oppressive, non-guilt-inflicting manner is the kind of teaching about social justice that is needed in many areas, the kind of approach that can begin to make our culture more humane for everyone. But a teacher or a parent has to be rather skillful to educate for justice in that way.

Over the past 20 years, from the time I signed my first statement against nuclear testing and, later, joined a picket line against segregation at a local movie theater, I have learned a few things about working for social justice from people long involved in similar issues. I pass them along in the hope that failure as well as success may be useful to others striving to embody the social teachings of the church. Or as my friend Mary Gleason, mother of six, put it: "Oh, I understand; you are going to tell about what we, as parents, tried to teach and how it all went awry."

The statement by the 1971 Synod of Bishops, *Justice in the World,* has been a guide to me. It speaks of "a new awareness which shakes people out of any fatalistic resignation and which spurs them on to liberate themselves and to be responsible for their own destiny." In such cases, the statement continues, "they express hope in a better world and a will to change whatever has become intolerable."

Some religious traditions—the Quakers, Mennonites, and other peace churches—have given these social concerns a central place from the beginning, that is, from the 17th and 18th centuries. Social concerns have re-emerged for Catholics by way of Leo XIII's encyclical *Rerum Novarum* (On the Condition of the Working Classes, 1891), Pius XI's *Quadragesimo Anno* (Social Reconstruction, 1931), *Mater et Magistra* (Christianity and Social Progress, 1961) and *Pacem in Terris* (Peace on Earth, 1963) by John XXIII, Paul VI's letter *Octogesima Adventiens* (A Call to Action: Letter on the 80th Anniversary of *Rerum Novarum*, 1971), and John Paul II's encyclical *Laborem Exercens* (Performing Work, 1981). In this sense, the emphasis upon social justice is new to American Catholicism. This book is both a reflection of and, I hope, a contribution to that movement.

Just so the reader will know: I have six children, ranging in age from 15 to 22—including three sons of draft age who have all struggled with how they will stand in relation to war. All of our children were young during the war in Indochina when my wife and I were involved in the anti-war movement, including the early years when most of the country (and the neighborhood) supported the policies of the American government. I have never written to see if the Federal Bureau of Investigation or the Central Intelligence Agency were watching us, but we were harassed by the Internal Revenue Service for refusing to pay part of our taxes. The local agent came to our house when we were not home and embarrassed the children in front of their friends by asking personal questions about the value of our car, whether it was paid for, and so on.

I say these things simply to suggest that, in dealing with problems of peace and justice, I speak from experience. For this reason, also, I have tried to be direct and modest, but at the same time tentative and open about ways of proceeding. A person doesn't have to be a parent of teenage children long to appreciate the fact that only luck and probably someone else's prayers carry one through at times. One of my wise contemporaries (father to a brood) had this advice: "When your children finally make it to adulthood, take none of the credit and none of the blame."

This is a book, finally, for concerned families whose contributions to peace and justice are as essential as anyone else's: the people on whom any movement for social justice is dependent in the long run.

1

The Dilemma

"Education for Justice is imparted first in the family."

Justice in the World, Synod of Bishops, 1971.

As a father I am particularly aware of the difficulties a man faces in talking about social justice with his children. The first reaction in thinking about the problem is this: Isn't it difficult enough just trying to keep them clothed, healthy, and out of trouble? Why complicate matters further by raising questions about war, poverty, and human rights? Won't this simply add to their sense of insecurity in a world that is often competitive, violent, and threatening already?

And, yes, raising these issues in the home is difficult. That is why it is important to give some thought to how it might be done. As in all other areas of parental guidance, actions speak louder than words, but a discussion of social justice at home where children feel free to question and to disagree is the best possible preparation for dealing with it outside the home—in the classroom or on the playground or, later, at work.

Conflict is as basic to family life as eating, drinking, and diapering, and it presents itself for discussion, even argument, from the time children are very young. Who first hit whom? or Who *did* kick the neighbor's cat? are questions as relevant to peace and justice as questions about border disputes at the United Nations. Probably parents won't

stress those similarities at the dinner table, while one an-
tagonist is still in a high chair and the other is learning to
talk. But within a short time, parents can.

Conflict resolution by nonviolent means is the technical
term for settling disputes at the national and international
levels. On most days that theory has immediate applica-
tions at home, and parents are wise to apply the theory as
opportunities present themselves.

Here as elsewhere, *not* raising the issues in the home
may leave the child unprepared for the future when decisions about such matters seem inevitable. What are the
awesome consequences, both moral and spiritual, if parents
do *not* encourage their children to make choices on the
side of honesty and charity? What will happen to them if
children are *not* taught the skills to live as responsible
people in the face of injustice?

Our concerns as religious people about how life should
be lived and to what purpose lead naturally, in light of
recent church teachings, to reflection on matters of public
interest. For the past 20 years the church has urged nations to stop manufacturing nuclear weapons. If using
them is evil, Paul VI said, so is making them, since it deprives hungry and homeless people of the resources
wasted in the process. Such teachings grow naturally out of
a reading of the Old Testament prophets, the life of Jesus,
and the corporal works of mercy.

Parents can choose passages almost at random from recent statements by the popes and American bishops that
dramatize the intimate relationship between their religious
beliefs and their responsibilities as citizens. "Action on behalf of justice and participation in the transformation of
the world fully appear to us," wrote the U.S. bishops in

Justice in the World (1971), "as a constitutive dimension of the preaching of the Gospel, or, in other words, of the church's mission for the redemption of the human race and its liberation from every oppressive situation."

It is one thing to hear these noble words (and agree with them as an adult Catholic); it is another, more difficult matter to assimilate them and practice what they preach (that is, to make them a part of life as a parent).

How does the phrase "liberation from every oppressive situation" apply, for example, to the division of labor in the family? How can a parent hear it and not think about the injustice of one person being stuck with all the cooking, all the cleaning, all the child care; or about the unfairness of young adults not working to help pay family bills? Similarly, how can a parent read about oppression and not think of American economic and foreign policies that perpetuate injustices in Central America or among migrant workers here in the U.S.?

Altering the structures that make such injustices inevitable is not easy, however, and the demanding tasks of raising a family leave little time and energy for "social causes." One example: About ten years ago, when five of her children were between the ages of 13 and 19, a friend told me that she had quit answering the telephone in the morning. An attentive, thoughtful, and faithful mother, she simply drew the line at that point, to make sure that she had enough energy to carry out the other principal tasks of "being there" for the family. She had learned from past experience, she said, that anyone who called the house before noon was (a) a guidance counselor complaining about an unexplained absence by one of her sons; (b) a cranky neighbor saying that another child, with a gang of rowdies, had walked across his yard on the way to school; or (c) a doctor or a dentist's office wondering why she hadn't sent in the payment for last month's (or the last six months') bill.

Why answer the telephone, she asked, when it meant only a further drain on the limited energy available to her in fulfilling the daily responsibilities of motherhood? This conflict (and I realize I am passing over a multitude of other justice issues raised by this incident) came at a time when this woman, her husband, and their family were trying hard to live the social teachings of the church in an exemplary fashion. She and her husband had followed one aspect of that teaching conscientiously, as they understood it, in having a large family in the first place. Later, in an effort to uphold other Christian values, they were active in the civil-rights movement, helped to establish a family discussion group around the teachings of Vatican II, and regularly made their home available to people in need.

And I must be frank about it: They sometimes got little support from the institutional church in fulfilling their responsibilities as parents. In that tough terrain where families are supposed to make the life and history of the church a part of everyday living, they felt rather isolated. At the very time they were trying to live out what the church taught about peace and justice, the clergy seldom spoke from the pulpit about those teachings and even regarded people attending to those demands of their faith as somewhat less than orthodox.

That situation has changed somewhat over the past decade. And many of the values that my friend and her family embody now provide topics for homilies against racism, for articles in the diocesan newspaper on nuclear disarmament, and for institutes in Catholic schools and colleges on hunger and violence. The oldest of their nine children grew up, nonetheless, without the institutional support they needed during the critical teenage years, placing heavy burdens on the parents to make a go of it on their own.

I mention this history not to blame anyone, including the institutional church, but merely to be accurate and fair about the complicating factors that parents deal with in all aspects of parenting, including social values. In caring for children, parents have to depend on many people, particularly as children grow older and increasingly independent, as they move into middle school, junior high, and high school. At those critical stages, the church sometimes provides little support for those most committed to its teachings. It remains, in many areas, quite aloof from the daily problems of child rearing.

I am not saying that the institutional church is not helpful in upholding basic Christian values. I am simply saying that celibate clergymen, in most of their administrative and educational roles, neither are nor can be aware of what it means to be a parent with two or three or four teenage children or of the psychological turmoil attending that critical stage of family life.

It is also often easier to work for justice outside the home than to create a just environment within the family. I have known days when handing out leaflets against non-union lettuce at the local supermarket looked a lot simpler than staying home and caring for six small children. Fulfilling one responsibility is not an excuse for evading the other. But doing both takes some setting of priorities, with justice demanding that on many days when I want to work elsewhere I have to remain at home. Such conflicts over time and energy are problems for everyone, and there are no easy solutions.

As in all matters of faith, parents need thoughtful, prayerful reflection, in trying to do the best they can as parents informed by church teachings. They must recognize, as well, that in social justice the leadership and the responsibilities are inevitably carried by the laity. In *Mater et Magistra,* John XXIII appeared to have this fact very much in mind when he spoke of the need for a qualified laity to put "the norms of instruction" into practice.

Teaching children these norms requires first of all a closer look at the way matters of justice work themselves out in the family: whether work loads are shared by all members, adults and children; whether everyone has a voice in making decisions; how commitment to resisting injustice outside the home flows from attention to the way time, energy, and money are spent inside the home. A dedication to nonviolence, for example, often means a resistance to the violence inherent in social structures, including the American family.

I have become particularly aware of the difficulty that fathers have in changing the role of authoritarian head of household they inherited in a patriarchal system. Most men, unless they were lucky enough to have a just but gentle father, are severely handicapped in this role. In the midst of job pressures and family responsibilities, it is easier to do the expected thing than to try to develop other more just and reasonable ways of being a parent.

How infrequently, for example, do men talk about the matter of being a father or discuss the conflicting feelings that the vocation brings with it: how alien men sometimes feel toward their own children during their early months; how feelings of jealousy or resentment mix with feelings of love and nurturing from the very beginning? Men are also much more reticent about discussing aspects of child care or about asking for advice from others about inevitable conflicts between parents and children. I am not certain of the causes for this particular kind of self-reliance (or non-cooperation), but it probably has something to do with a style of patriarchy whereby a man was supposed to be a great repository of truth and wisdom and knowledge about practically everything. Ignorance may have been regarded as a sign of weakness or unmanliness. Perhaps men were just so far removed from the daily trials of child rearing that they never considered dealing with such basic questions. Worse perhaps, they were never around.

I am as a man only partially aware of the difficulties that mothers face in changing an inequitable system they inherited. I assumed that women were much less handicapped than men in their preparation for parenthood. My impression was that women talked to one another more naturally about what parenting is about. They seemed franker about the basic aspects of child care, from feeding to diapering, and about maintaining dialogue with young children on a wide range of subjects. Only men, I thought, had to learn about such basic aspects of child rearing "on the firing line," with every skill similarly undeveloped and restricted.

Some of my perceptions were accurate, no doubt, but one of my friends who should know, as a mother and a social psychologist, says that many women feel as unprepared for and uncomfortable with parenting as men. "In addition, because people usually subscribe to the assumption that women are better prepared," she says, "any attempt by women to describe the conflicts admitted by men are met with disbelief. Men may regard the admission of inadequacy as revelations, as consciousness raising, as positive; women commonly look upon them, in relation to themselves, as confessions of incompetence or with guilt."

Is this not further evidence of the need to prepare both mothers and fathers for child care and to support them in the process? And doesn't it illustrate the need, as well, to distribute the work of child care more equitably and to raise its status?

In our culture, perhaps especially among men, child care has seldom been recognized or rewarded as an occupation that requires all the energy, talent, and intelligence a parent can muster.

But is there any work more difficult than the juggling act performed by most mothers and some fathers on an ordinary morning around the breakfast table: feeding a baby perhaps only recently weaned to table food, while answering the ten-a-minute questions of an ordinary 3-year-old, in the midst of settling a quarrel between two 10-year-olds (your own and a troublesome neighbor's)—all at the same time. How many people are flexible or intelligent enough, really, to keep three dialogues going, at three different stages of development, among those children? Yet family teaching and learning about peace and justice takes place here.

These things may seem very distant from the problems of teaching social justice, but I think they are not, and it is important to mention them, in passing, before going on to the more rational concerns that parents face. These irrational considerations arise because of the nature of the family as a community. Here children have their first experience with how people react to one another: how love is expressed; how conflicts are resolved; how decisions are made, and how work is allocated. There is no set formula for handling any of these matters, no best way for everyone. And what is done will vary greatly, depending upon the needs and gifts and personalities of different people. But if peace and justice are to have some priority in a community of people some attention must be given to the way in which these questions are addressed.

Parents sometimes address the questions before children arrive on the scene, but probably—given the nature of our society—they are never settled. Parents struggle with them again in every new stage of development in children and in each of the passages through which they move toward adulthood. A person's development is never static, and to speak about social justice is to speak inevitably about religious and spiritual matters.

The point is that the ways in which a husband and wife deal with the simplest household matters raise questions about social justice, and that it is important for them to make decisions about where they stand. They do not have to agree or even be at the same point in their interest in, understanding of, or commitment to social justice. This can vary in each individual, depending upon family background, education, and personal involvement over a period of years. But one parent cannot carry all the burdens of the household, for example, while the other involves himself or herself in activities outside the home. Unless such matters are discussed and arranged to the satisfaction of both, the parent staying at home rightly becomes resentful. Reflection and a lot of practice go into solving this problem. In recent years, it has become increasingly common for peace and justice groups to provide child care during meetings or actions so that a husband or a wife or a single parent is not excluded from participating. That is the kind of informed and practical solution needed all along the line.

Working for peace and justice includes doing whatever is needed, including sharing basic family chores, to strengthen the bonds of the family and to avoid unnecessary conflict in a marriage. There are already many forces—economic, social, and political—that pose serious threats to enduring human relationships in American culture. A husband and wife are wise then to make preparations, even before children arrive on the scene, to see that education and action for social justice is a sustaining rather than a threatening factor in the family.

CHILDREN

Children are the great humanizing factor in life, bringing a note of reality to any theoretical discussion. They quickly expose the weakness of many philosophical positions and the vagueness of unwarranted assumptions. Their needs are so great and so persistent that parents cannot simply set them aside or postpone addressing them without missing useful insights into the behavior, thoughts, and feelings of the children.

A colleague of mine stressed this in talking about her four children and how much she learned about them in conversations right after their coming home from school. One by one, several minutes apart, they talked with her about homework or classes or conversations during the day. Things that they were hesitant to discuss at the dinner table in front of the other children came up quite naturally in those daily tête-à-têtes. Later, when she began to teach and no adult was home after school, she and her husband heard less about the children's feelings and thoughts on many subjects.

My own education on the importance of listening to children took some time, my inclination being to set that aside in favor of "more important matters." I remember a conversation with my brother, whose children are just enough older than ours to have educated him and then me to attend to their needs more conscientiously than I might have. One early morning at the Raleigh-Durham airport he said something very wise, after I had just complained, in a loud, strained voice, to our young son and daughter: "Be quiet and behave yourselves. This is one of the few moments we have with your uncle, and I don't want it ruined by your talking and running around and asking questions." At that point, Herb turned to me and said, gently but firmly: "Now, wait a minute. I think you have to realize that our conversation must include them and that they are a part of almost everything you're involved in from now on. Besides, I'm here to visit them, too."

Work for social justice is best seen in that light, as part of, not in addition to, or in conflict with, raising a family. But with the pressures of time, limitations of energy, and lack of support from the institutions that impinge on our lives, it is often difficult to keep that perspective.

Peace and justice, like everything parents teach their children, are best approached with an eye toward the stages of development of the child. Just as learning languages and mathematics—striking a balance between concreteness and abstraction—depends to a degree on the age and maturity of the child, so do matters of social justice.

15

Children have specific needs and insecurities at different ages which can influence how and when they react to certain values. Peace and justice are weighty matters. It is important to not overwhelm children at a particular time and to always attend to the way they respond. Injustice is a fact of life and a persistent theme in children's literature—nursery rhymes and fairy tales. So are violence and struggle. I am not suggesting, therefore, that parents protect children from the harsh realities of the world, only that they try to be aware of and attentive to their reactions.

I was surprised to learn, for example, how much our children resented my inviting visitors home at suppertime, people from work or nearby towns. Since mealtime was often the only time we were together as a family, the children were jealous of the time and attention directed at someone else. Sympathetic as I was to their complaint, I did not think, however, that they should set the policy for everyone. The ensuing discussion was revealing and helpful in deciding on how to proceed on a policy involving the whole group. Some visitors ignored the children, who were quick to point out how demeaning that was for them. This led into a longer discussion of how a person upholds his or her own in such circumstances, without being abusive or insensitive in return. Visitors frequently raise questions about conflicts among individuals and families, many of them related to peace and justice.

Once children become teenagers, they will probably be quite public about what they think about their parents' system of values (and almost inevitably rebel against them). Younger children seldom state their position directly, although they may lock memories about important discussions away for later reference.

The experience of one of my students is pertinent here. Now 22 years old and about to graduate from college, he described a particularly difficult time in his life. When he was 10, his father, a city alderman, was severely criticized for taking a stand against a powerful industrialist on a building proposal in his home town. There were anonymous phone calls and unkind remarks from schoolmates, and the young boy was torn between loyalty to his father and his own fear of being unpopular with the crowd. It was only years later that he looked back with pride at his father's courage in doing what was best for the community. Eventually everyone in town understood that, too, and the young college student now appreciates his father's willingness to take a stand—something that, as a young child, brought only confusion and resentment.

But perhaps this example is too dramatic or public. Most of the realities about justice are much less striking and probably have to do with such mundane matters as how to treat a hostile neighbor or the new person on the block, how to respond in the classroom to a slur about Jews or blacks or Puerto Ricans, or how to deal with the prejudices of the school yard or playground. All the issues written large in the daily headlines seem to come up eventually at the supper table or more likely in the casual remarks of children at the moment parents least expect them.

It was long after the death of President John Kennedy, for example, that my wife and I learned what a deep effect that assassination had on one of our children who was 3 years old at the time. Whenever we left the house, the child got anxious or cried, fearful, he told us years later, that one of us might be shot on the street. With children, issues come together in strange combinations, producing an ef-

17

fect that parents may understand only long afterward. And the implications of what parents say may return to haunt them in unexpected ways.

I was reminded of this recently as I faced the annual defeat of filing tax payments for the April 15 deadline. The Internal Revenue Service had just seized money from my pay check. (We had refused to pay part of our bill the year before.) How infuriating and demoralizing, I thought, knowing that half of our taxes go not to feed and clothe the poor but to buy more bombs and bombers to be used against them!

At that very moment, my 16-year-old son came to ask me if he could borrow some money to take a long trip West, to attend a national antidraft conference for high-school and college students from around the country. There *he* was living out the very values that he had learned at home, only to raise further anxieties in me about how deeply I wanted him to be involved in draft resistance. I found myself counseling caution, while thinking at the same time about ways of confronting militarism more directly.

But I, of course, have much more experience than my son does. I have seen young men and women in the past move too quickly into radical positions without the sustaining power of prayer, reflection, and community support.

Young people, particularly, need support and skills to make their way in the world. It is one thing to face unsympathetic neighbors and co-workers (or the courtroom) if a person has thought through and chosen a position from among a variety of possibilities. It is quite another to face the same conditions without the experience of stating that position for oneself and for others. For this reason I am wary of adults with a certain charisma who encourage rebellion among the young and then abandon them when they need support. Becoming an adult is a long and complex process, and parents' concern for their children rightfully leads them to be very attentive to the ways in which their values exhibit themselves in action.

Thinking ahead is important for two reasons. First, parents are tempted not to take a stand for fear of the consequences to their family. Some people will, in fact, punish parents for speaking out: "They must be totally thoughtless, refusing to pay taxes (or taking a public stand against the draft). Think of the poor children!" People who say such things seldom consider the consequences to children when parents willingly pay taxes for bombs leading to everyone's destruction. This sentence, from Henry David Thoreau's *Civil Disobedience,* is appropriate here: "If a thousand men were not to pay their tax bills this year, that would not be as violent and bloody a measure as it would be to pay them and enable the state to commit violence and shed innocent blood."

The second reason for considering how children carry out their values has to do with trusting them to solve personal and social conflicts on their own. Children do have strengths to handle conflict, and if the stress is not too great they often carry through with remarkable imagination and effectiveness. Our 8-year-old son faced such a conflict with a lawyer on his paper route several years ago over the Vietnam War. Asked why he opposed American policy in Southeast Asia, the boy surprised himself, I think, in presenting his reasons for doing so, never having had to defend that position to an adult before. He may not have convinced that lawyer or changed his mind on the issue,

but he did win the man's respect, which grew to a friendship in subsequent years.

When raising children in a home where social justice is
central to family life, parents do have to be prepared for
harder conflicts as well. Not all neighbors are as tolerant or
reasonable as the lawyer I just mentioned.

We had another neighbor whose capacity for cruelty to
children seemed boundless. We were first alerted to her
particular brand of child harassment when she told our
2-year-old son she was going to call the police on him for
running his toy truck off the sidewalk and into her flower
bed. Later, confrontations between her and the children
proved to be more serious, many of them provoked, no
doubt, by the disparity between her defining the church in
alliance with Holy Mother the State, and our viewing it as
an institution in conflict with the state.

The result was a late afternoon visit, when I had to tell
her to bring her insults directly to us, not to the children, if
she disagreed with our way of being in the world. Her
subsequent behavior was as insufferable as it had been for
years, but she did change her way of dealing with the
children. She is even occasionally kind to them, in fact, in
their capacity as paper-carriers in the neighborhood.

If children learn to deal with people and conflicts of this
kind it is a useful introduction to the risks they will face
later on, testing their powers of faith and endurance in
small but significant ways. Conflict resolution is also part
of family life. The nuances and textures of basic human
relationships are the very heart of family existence and,
therefore, of the whole process of teaching about social
justice.

With violence all around, how do parents teach that violence need not be the first response to conflict? In a world filled with hungry people, how do parents teach children that sharing food and resources is a matter not of charity, but of justice? And in a culture that is often indifferent to such questions, how do parents encourage such realizations without making children feel merely guilty or powerless to change things?

These questions present themselves in the most unexpected ways in the family, from the time children are very young and in the midst of complicated circumstances. What does a parent do, for example, about guns or war toys? If a parent refuses to buy them, the inventive little rascals construct them out of sticks or scraps of metal, and if neither of those materials are handy, they soon discover that the thumb and forefinger, properly cocked, will serve. (My own recommendation is, nonetheless, to hold the line on toy guns as long as possible.) In the face of peer and commercial pressure, a bit of nonviolent resistance on the part of parents works occasionally.

But likely as not any simple solution gets undermined in other ways. The experience of the mother of a 10-year-old boy is representative and characteristically complex. She and her husband refuse to allow their son to own a toy gun, but his grandfather periodically invites the boy to go on hunting trips with him. Eventually, the older man will encourage the boy to learn the skills of the master. Where will the mother draw the line: refuse to allow her son to go with his grandfather, thus depriving him of the company of a person he loves, or risk another argument with her father over conflicting values and hope for the best? Actually, she hasn't decided *what* she will do, but the ensuing years will undoubtedly find her facing many of the basic

21

dilemmas of peace and justice, with implications in the family as well as in the wider community.

Once children are in school, the complications increase because additional people are involved—teachers, administrators, and classmates. Adults, including teachers, who might otherwise be reluctant to criticize parents will occasionally taunt children with whom they disagree. What does a parent do then: confront the teacher or neighbor and perhaps bring down further sanctions against the child or listen carefully, pray a lot, and trust the child to handle the situation alone?

At such moments I remember those black children in southern schools during the early days of the civil-rights movement and afterward who faced similar situations daily. Their stories, told in Robert Coles's *Children of Crisis: Volume I, A Study of Courage and Fear,* are an essential part of that struggle. In the midst of potentially violent confrontations, the children remained calm and determined, and their behavior is a model for anyone seeking to resolve conflict through nonviolent means.

If parents are serious about upholding social justice, they need to prepare themselves for that kind of dilemma. They need to keep themselves aware of the issues and try to give their children the necessary skills to face that dilemma themselves.

2

Family Awareness

"Values cannot be taught as such; they can only be assimilated. The process is essentially one of exploration by the child, learning through personal experience and, above all, personal involvement."

Norman J. Bull, 1969

All the subtleties of being a mother and father are required in teaching children to uphold peace and justice. It means being as aware and involved as energy allows. This awareness is accomplished in a variety of ways, but principally through the value system that permeates the home. Children are like little Geiger counters in their manner of measuring, moment by moment, the waves that strike them. Is there anything more interesting and surprising than their method of picking up signals from parents or other elders and storing them for future reference?

As a teacher, I am constantly amazed at what students remember, for example, from a particular class or course. Years later, they will mention this or that discussion or remark, made in passing, only tangentially related to the reading or lecture of the day. A point struck them, sometimes, because it addressed an issue confronting them in daily life. In a discussion of a poem by T. S. Eliot or a story by Ernest Hemingway, they remember a reference to Eliot's own religious quest or Hemingway's conflict with his mother, long after they have forgotten "The Love Song

of J. Alfred Prufrock" or "A Clean Well-lighted Place."
When I hear them repeat what they heard, I am often
tempted to repeat the lines from Eliot's poem: "That is not
what I meant at all. . . . That is not it at all."

The same holds true for children. They, too, remember
events and record impressions that influence their moral
development in ways that mothers and fathers never in-
tend. Parents do well, therefore, to make certain truths, in
this case the social teachings of the church, concrete in
several ways—not only in how they conduct their own
lives, but also through personal associations and, as much
as possible, through the stories of heroes and heroines of
peace and justice.

This teaching is part of the moral education of children,
a large topic and the subject of numerous studies based
upon various theories of human development. The
theories of Jean Piaget have been particularly influential,
his approach suggesting the sequences through which a
child travels on the road to moral maturity. Later writers,
including Erik Erickson and Norman J. Bull, have further
defined these stages, with the latter's *Moral Education* identifying them roughly in the following manner: childhood,
ages 4–9; the middle years, 9–13; and adolescence, 13–18.

This does not mean that nothing happens in education
for justice before the age of 4. Far from it, as a recent Lynn
Johnston comic strip, "For Better or For Worse," indicated. The seven frames in the sequence pictured a
mother, a toddler, and a preschool child in familiar family
scenes. The opening frames carry a series of brief
monologues by the children: (1) "Ma, Lizzie *hit* me!" (2)
"But he took my *bunny!*"—followed by (3) "She broke my
house"; "He bited my dolly"; and "But she. . . ." At this

point, the harried mother shouts, "Hold it! Since I cannot possibly know who's at fault here, you can both go to your rooms for 20 minutes. . . ." Then, exhausted, slumped in a chair, the mother thinks to herself, ". . . so the judge and the jury may enjoy a brief recess."

Up through the age of 4, the judge-and-jury (that is, the parent looking after the child most of the time) dispenses peace and justice while making a hundred other rulings essential to the survival of the human family. Perhaps the Nobel Committee should establish a special peace prize for veterans of those campaigns.

A parent deals with many things at once in teaching children during the period called the early or premoral stage of development. The mother of three children stressed this recently when I asked her about how she went about teaching peace and justice to children between 4 and 9 years of age. "Children must be taught to be honest," she began without hesitation. "And I don't mean just with money. Many people are inclined to do something for convenience's sake, when it should be done another way."

An incident that made an impression on one of her children, she mentioned by way of example, was the mother's fair treatment of a person on the block whom the child knew she disliked and, in truth, didn't trust. But in upholding a principle of justice even with a reputedly unjust person, the mother conveyed a truth that no amount of preaching or Bible texting could have accomplished.

"Take advantage of things as they come up in the news," she said, "because it doesn't work to bring them up out of the blue or to raise an issue at the parent's convenience." The daily paper, news programs, or conflicts with teachers and schoolmates, at games or play, almost inevitably center on questions about giving people their due. "The problem is not to shield children from injustice and violence (because you can't anyway), but to make them thoughtful about such things," she concluded.

At some stages of development, especially in the middle years, children can be very conformist about social values. They do not want their parents to be different, and they do not want to be different themselves. Although I did not realize it at the time, the behavior of our son who wanted us to be *more* rather than less materialistic was characteristic of most children his age. The middle years are a time when children develop a strong sense of what is fair or unfair; and, indeed, our child's criticism of us, because we did not deliver "the goodies" that some of his contemporaries enjoyed, was a kind of protest against life's unfairness to him.

Fiction for young children often provides a good dramatization of social justice problems. In the early years, simple plots, with plenty of action, particularly stories about real children and real places, attract young readers. The books (not the television adaptations, which are different) of Laura Ingalls Wilder are obviously popular for this reason. Parents may also wish to adapt the marvelous stories of Robert Coles's *Children of Crisis* series or various tales about Thomas Paine and similar historical figures.

At this stage of development, a child needs to learn that moral education is open-ended, as Norman Bull says, and that genuine morality requires free choice rather than mere slavish imitation. That is a tough perspective to maintain in all circumstances. This principle haunted me years ago, I remember, regarding a promise I made to one of the children about getting a pet.

In early January, I had said "No!" to the original request, thinking at the time that all we needed to upset the precarious balance in our household between organized chaos and complete disaster was another boarder of any kind. "How about this summer," my son went on to say, "when I can train the dog myself. May I get one then?" "But if we go to Minnesota on vacation, who will take care of it?" I asked, seeing the possibility of a reprieve. Next question: "And if we don't go to Minnesota this summer, then can I get a dog?" "Yes," I answered, "but not until after school is out."

Six months later, my son still remembered the conversation and the promise that I had conveniently forgotten. On the closing day of school, he rode 14 miles by bicycle to pick up a $5.00 black Labrador, which is still with us. It was a hard lesson for me; but justice, alas, was upheld.

In early adolescence, the complications involved in teaching social justice or any other value multiply a hundredfold (with reference to sex, drugs, the draft, etc.). It is also, psychologists tell us, "the time of greatest development in moral judgment." Helping children through this period (as well as surviving it themselves) can test the physical, spiritual, and psychological strength of the heartiest parents. I have seen more than one person undone by these turbulent years.

Frequently, also, the values that parents taught in one context return, in the behavior of older children, in very different guises. This is particularly true of religious values. In one family, for example, parents taught their religious values by requiring their children to go to Mass every Sunday, perfectly groomed and seated in the front row. In late adolescence, these children, in characteristic rebellion, refused to attend church regularly. At the same time, the deeper truths they learned—respect for life and commitment to the welfare of others—mark them as some of the most genuinely moral young adults I know.

From the time children are 13 through to maturity, parents' dependence upon outside help—the support of the church, school, neighbors, and the community—is very great. In facing the challenges of teaching values in these critical years, I have been sustained at times by the remark of my friend, mother of six, ages 16–24. "The word for parents of late adolescents in the 1980s," she said, "is *hang in there.*" This means that mothers and fathers should not give up on teaching essential values or, in their children's eyes, being wrong, even when their offspring appear to ignore them during the high school and college years. As adolescence in America stretches into the early 20s and as young people postpone marriage and having children later and later, they appear to be less concerned about some religious and moral questions that earlier generations settled at an early age.

Remember, however, that these young people have grown up in a period when many questions about personal morality, particularly sexuality, and public responsibility have been re-examined with considerable intensity, if infrequent rationality. Since 1960 they have been subjected to many mixed messages, not only in the public order (the Indochina war, Watergate, and the new conservatism) but also in the home. In a country where many children live with parents in the midst of arranging a divorce or in single-parent homes, they are quite understandably unsure about an older generation's thoughts and feelings on the nature of family life. Their confusion is sometimes carried over into the adolescents' concern or lack of concern about social life and the public order.

As my children get older, I find them and their friends exceedingly curious about what parents think about religious issues, including those I thought we were quite clear about. I am not saying that they always take on our views or act as we wish. But they do indicate in various ways that they want to hear concrete rationales and to see specific actions that clarify the issues. Anxious to point out inconsistencies among religious people, particularly, they are surprised and pleased to learn of the public statements and actions of clergy and laity, including the American bishops, about social issues that touch on their future. How helpful it is, as a parent, to be able to point to an editorial, like the following, that appeared in the local diocesan newspaper in response to President Reagan's policy on the neutron bomb:

> America's "Pro-Life President" took another giant step this week toward eliminating abortions.
>
> He authorized development of neutron warheads which would eliminate people.
>
> Oh, yes, the building will remain—and the tanks that the dead soldiers were riding.
>
> But there will be no mothers and fathers to do that deed that would require the decision to have or not have that child.

And that insightful woman mentioned earlier was right in suggesting that on days when parents least expect it, something of what they tried to teach children about honesty, justice, or nonviolence exhibits itself: Their children give money to a stranger in need; defend an unpopular person or cause; or take a job, with less pay, in the service of others.

Even the recommended models get a hearing, on occasion. Last fall, during the first month of college, our son called home to talk about his courses, including the required one in religion (which he would not have signed up for voluntarily). He had once referred to the Plowshares 8—the eight peace activists who had damaged missile nosecones at a General Electric plant—whom we admire, as "mere troublemakers." He surprised us by announcing that his religion professor often mentioned "those people" favorably in class. "And you know," he added, with an innocence and authority that only a freshman possesses, "they're really *important.*"

In other words, a few of these values have taken root in our family, sometimes by accident and other times by planning. In most cases, we managed much less structuring—a central requirement in any education— than I wished. But with children close together, there is not always time for that. Again, the company one keeps provides a life-saving support system.

One of the families we celebrate July 4th with, for example, always reads the Declaration of Independence after the family picnic that day, with each person around the table taking a paragraph. Hearing Thomas Jefferson's noble words about the right to revolution and the duty to resist injustice made a deep impression on our children, even as they balked at reading aloud in front of others. That ringing call to life and liberty, reminding people of their right to rebel when oppression is great and unendurable, surprised them. Young people hearing those words may yet be inspired to recall the United States to its proper history or at least to remember a noble moment in its past.

It is valuable, also, to have biographies and collections of essays on hand when children need suggestions for class reports and projects. There are obviously many such books to choose from, and I don't wish to simply list them without comment in a long bibliography, nor do I want to set down the names that have not stood the test of experience. But in the chapter on resources I do list a selected group, in addition to those mentioned elsewhere in this book.

I list these books not merely because they deal with peace and justice, but because they present them through the lives of very human people—Anne Frank, young Catholic workers, and ordinary people with whom young readers can identify. My standard of evaluation is not my own, but that of my children and their friends—severe critics all, who refuse to read any book that does not hold their attention. Generally speaking, they despise writing that is preachy or moralistic and, therefore, boring. Rest assured that any book on my list made it past the dragon, so to speak, of the children's critics circle.

There is a great need in American culture, which is both dynamic and forgetful—alive to the possibilities of the present, but destructive of the achievements of the past—to remind young people of what has gone before. The best way to remember the past is to tell stories and anecdotes that dramatize people's courage and determination in the face of oppression. This is equally true of the saints, those generous, peculiar, and intelligent men and women whose lives, as John Henry Newman once wrote, are "the most complete and logical evidence" of Christianity. "In a saint's thoughts, words, acts, trials, fortunes, beginnings, and growth, there is a divine influence and persuasion, a power of exercising and eliciting the latent elements of divine grace in individual readers, as no other reading can claim." What Newman said of the saints can be said of the great apostles of nonviolence, including men and women in recent history who have devoted themselves persistently to social justice.

For those who maintain that social justice is a political rather than a religious concern, it is necessary to point to an older tradition that says they belong together. I am thinking here of the corporal and spiritual works of mercy, based upon biblical teachings of the Old as well as the New Testament.

The Old Testament is filled with references to peace and justice, whereby God insists upon concern for the poor and proper stewardship of the goods of the earth. Isaiah, Jeremiah, and Ezekiel, as well as Proverbs, emphasize God's counsel on the relationship between good works and worship, and there are numerous other counsels, particularly the Sermon on the Mount and the letters of the Apostles after the death of Jesus.

Over the centuries, these counsels of justice, recommended by the Prophets and central to the Gospels, became a tradition within the church. By the Middle Ages, the works of mercy, based upon those counsels, provided themes and subject matter for the work of artists and writers. The list of corporal works of mercy is long established, with the seven spiritual works of mercy developing from them.

The corporal works are directed toward the public order and are therefore particularly pertinent to social teachings. The spiritual works, which deal more with personal relationships, seem appropriate, also, at a time when such relationships in the family and the wider community are uncertain and when people's sense of belonging is rather fragile.

These works have a particular relevance, in other words, to the family and social justice. And a handsomely lettered poster or an enlargement of the skillful calligraphy periodically reprinted in the *Catholic Worker* is an effective way of calling attention to their counsels:

Corporal works of mercy	*Spiritual works of mercy*
1. Feed the hungry.	1. Instruct the ignorant.
2. Give drink to the thirsty.	2. Counsel the doubtful.
3. Clothe the naked.	3. Admonish the sinner.
4. Shelter the homeless.	4. Bear wrongs patiently.
5. Visit the sick.	5. Forgive offenses.
6. Ransom the captive.	6. Comfort the afflicted.
7. Bury the dead.	7. Pray for the living and the dead.

In a nuclear age, it seems only right and just to add another item to both lists: 8. Ban the bomb (corporal) and Support those who resist building the bomb (spiritual). If these works aren't performed by all of us, no one will be around to practice any of the others.

CITIZENSHIP

The importance of family awareness and citizen action for peace and justice perhaps can best be illustrated with the arms race. Following World War II, the U.S. emerged as the dominant military power, and since then the continuing pressure to look for military solutions to conflicts has led to the present standoff of mutual assured destruction (MAD).

This change in policy by the United States has been justified by every administration of the past 40 years, of whatever party or disposition. The policy is tolerated by the American people, accepted out of apathy, moral indifference, perhaps mere laziness. In a perceptive essay entitled "On the Ineffectuality of Certain Intelligent People," the late Paul Goodman, poet, psychologist, and educational philosopher, talked about this process whereby people fail to act on what they know to be true and good and right; and in *The Society I Live in Is Mine,* he made practical proposals for altering a bad situation.

Goodman explained the obligations of citizenship, of people acting as free men and women, in order to alter the direction of local and national policies. "It is appalling," Goodman said, "how few people regard themselves as citizens, as society-makers, in this existential sense. Rather, people seem to take society as a pre-established machinery of institutions and authorities, and they take themselves as I don't know what, some kind of individuals 'in' society, whatever that means. Such a view is dangerous because it must result in a few people being society makers and exercising power over the rest," and in a great deal of neglect, injustice, waste. The remedy is "large numbers of authentic citizens, alert, concerned, intervening, deciding, on all issues and at all levels." Parents would do well to remind themselves of such principles by keeping the writings of Paul Goodman nearby for challenge and inspiration.

Such calls for citizen participation are a common theme in the lives and writings of many Americans committed to social justice over the past three centuries. But it is also a persistent theme in Catholic social teachings in recent times. "Once again, we exhort our children to take an active part in public life and to contribute towards the attainment of the common good of the entire human family, as well as to that of their own country," John XXIII wrote in *Pacem in Terris.* In "The Call to Action," Paul VI declared, "The Christian has the duty to take part in the organization and life of political society." This was echoed five years later, in 1976, by the administrative board of the American bishops, in their bicentennial statement: "We need a committed, informed, and involved citizenry to revitalize our political life, to require accountability from our political leaders and governmental institutions and to achieve the common good."

The struggle for disarmament and a nuclear freeze in the United States is akin to the struggle for decent wages and the right to food, water, and education among the oppressed in the Third and Fourth World countries. At times the odds seem insurmountable. Yet people in this country, like peasants of Central and South America, must not remain submerged in the "culture of silence," failing to look critically at a desperate situation or to develop tools for repairing the damage being done. The world, as Goodman said, is not static, a closed order, and the present military establishment, spending something over $200 billion a year, is not permanent and inevitable. History is not yet at an end, as long as people are willing to commit themselves to revitalize it.

Parents must emphasize the positive nature of work for social justice. It is essential to say "No!" to injustice, to the forces of death, and to say "Yes!" to the forces of life. That means encouraging and helping to sustain every sign of renewal and rebirth. That is why celebration, including the Mass and other religious liturgies, is so much a part of "the new awareness" the papal encyclical speaks about.

Children placed continually in an environment of discouragement and depression cannot adopt a positive attitude toward life. And what is true of children is true of adults. I have always been amazed at people working for social change who spend half their time complaining about how few show up for meetings or turn out for a demonstration around the issues. My first thought on hearing that complaint, is, "Yes, you're right, and I should have stayed home, too, if my presence is worth so little."

Yes, of course, I wish thousands of people would show up at a parish meeting to discuss Catholic social teachings or at a school assembly on draft information. And when looking for volunteers to help with a benefit to provide food for the hungry or to aid refugees in Africa, I naturally like enthusiastic support from everyone. But if there are only five people, that's the place to begin, happy that five people have given their time, outside the regular routine of work, family, recreation.

One more note on the importance of sustained and positive thinking. I, at least, cannot work in an atmosphere where the talk is continually of impending disaster. Even though I believe the predictions that a nuclear war is practically inevitable within the next 20 years, insistence on that black future seldom provokes me to action. My mind rebels and my reaction is probably shared by many people. I think, "Well, if it's that certain that the apocalypse is here, then I might as well give up, join the passive majority, and quit wasting time working for social change."

People, young, old, or middle-aged, must think and feel

that, at some level, their efforts to make a better world (prayers, letters, vigils, meetings, demonstrations, sit-ins) are productive. They must have a sense that these are not just futile gestures in the face of impending doom. They have to have not only religious faith but also a kind of "animal faith" that the world is meant not only to survive but also to flourish and that "the Holy Ghost over the bent world broods with warm breast, and with ah! bright wings." In a post-Christian atomic age, that bird brooding over the world may resemble the pathetic critter described in Thomas Hardy's "The Darkling Thrush," more than the magnificent bird in Gerard Manley Hopkins' "God's Grandeur." But each image must be firmly fixed in the imagination of anyone who is conscious of what has happened to Western civilization since 1914. Both images are important, if one is to accurately assess the present reality or prospects for the future.

As a final note on family awareness, let me repeat: Celebrate around the struggles and victories, however small, of social justice—the passage of a bill in Congress, a positive vote by the state legislature on banning the manufacture of nuclear weapons, the anniversary of a peace and justice center in the local community. The church, a great teacher of the necessity of celebration, follows a liturgical calendar combining equal portions of instruction and festivity, mortification and consolation, *dies irae* and hallelujah. There is no sense in making work for social justice a perpetual exercise in crepe-hanging. No community of adults and children will form around a movement for social change that is half in love with death.

3

Justice

"Remove the chains of oppression and the yoke of injustice, and let the oppressed go free. Share your food with the hungry and open your homes to the homeless poor. Give clothes to those who have nothing to wear."

Isaiah 58:6-7

"To love God we must seek justice. To love our country we must seek to overcome the corporate government and military policies that victimize the bodies and spirits of people at home and abroad."

Jack Nelson, *Hunger for Justice*

Rearing children is a very difficult task, but it is difficult in ways that few people ever tell about in books. Perhaps that is so because many experts on the subject spend most of their time doing something called research rather than facing the day-to-day, moment-by-moment conflicts that arise in the care of children. Many books on rearing children have been written by theorists who make it all sound simple. And much of the writing about sexism, racism, and militarism lacks the sense of immediacy and the psychological cross currents of life as it is lived because it leaves out the children and the contexts in which these problems present themselves in the family.

Parents also must be clear about what the problems are in light of recent Catholic teachings and the signs of the times. With that dual purpose in mind, I will describe a few dilemmas that my family has struggled with, hoping that parents might be able to relate our family experiences to their own.

The term social justice, as it is used in recent Catholic teachings, deals with the nature of the whole social order—the relationship between children and parents, family and community, individual and the state. Earlier church teachings on justice usually were limited to the duties of love, recommending that people share their goods out of charity. What was once treated as a matter of charity is now regarded as a matter of obligation. "The demands of justice should be first satisfied," states the Vatican II Decree on the Apostolate of the Laity, "lest the giving of what is due" be represented as the offering of a gift.

Granting people their rights as human beings is no longer seen as a kind of almsgiving, whereby the rich and powerful allow others a modicum of human dignity. It is a duty in recognition of the rights of all. Catholic social teaching proclaims the right to "life, liberty, and the pursuit of happiness" to all nations, including those exploited by a few industrial economies.

This teaching regards anything that divides people unnecessarily or makes one group rich at the expense of another as a sin against the whole. The condemnation of war or racism or abortion is not, in other words, merely a sentimental preoccupation with one or two aspects of human existence but a recognition of the dignity of the individual on a broad scale. Debate continues around central questions such as at what point does a fetus become a human person, or when does a man or woman lose the right to life under the law. In all cases the church stresses the right of all persons to whatever is essential to their physical and spiritual development.

It is this commitment to the welfare of the individual as well as to the global community that provides the basis for the teachings on social justice. The next two chapters will focus on a few of these issues—hunger, sexism, and the draft—as they arise in the family.

Obviously such a list does not exhaust the social concerns of church teachings. The concerns of justice are constantly developing as part of the dynamic nature of the church. Over a century ago, in *An Essay on the Development of Christian Doctrine,* Cardinal John Henry Newman called attention to the gradual understanding of church teachings. All discussions of them are, in a sense, "essays" or "attempts" at understanding the fullness of God's message. That understanding is an evolutionary one, with each step toward peace and justice conditioned by what emerges at any historical moment.

One difficulty in maintaining a moral system in any age arises from the multiple responsibilities of parents, requiring them both to love their children, that is, give them a sense of security and self-regard, and to teach them, that is, make distinctions between good and bad. In the early years teaching children about good and bad is not so difficult, since their experience of the world is limited and their desire to please their parents is strong. Yet even then, in justice, parents must prepare them for the inevitable break, for the rebellion, for the freedom that allows them not only to choose but also to reject whatever values are important to their parents. Even then it is essential to show rather than merely to tell them that some values are better than others.

This task becomes increasingly demanding as children grow older, particularly as the pressures become almost overwhelming in contemporary American culture. How can parents convey to children that life is good, but that much that is rewarded in the marketplace is evil? How can parents say that competition and aggressiveness are bad, when they see the competitive instincts rewarded all around them and the cooperative instincts discouraged or ignored? What must children think of justice and peace, when the big salaries go not to the people promoting nutritious food or peaceful co-existence, but to those promoting chemically processed junk food and to others talking about the benefits of the neutron bomb?

Yet even when children take on the bad, the ways that often lead to success and power, parents cannot reject them. They have to keep working, praying, hoping, holding up other values and asserting that other choices exist. In all of this effort, the most obvious virtues are essential, as the mother quoted earlier made clear: "Children must be taught to be honest."

Being under children's scrutiny every moment of the day, parents are themselves often subjected to severe critical judgment, and as their sons and daughters get older, their awareness of the parents' inconsistencies becomes more and more acute. At the beginning, they are likely to accuse the parents of insincerity for associating with people whose values the parents once criticized or of not always living by the principles that were preached.

The task of teaching the basic virtues is not completed

by explaining them at age 4 or 10 or 15. In late adolescence, their rational arguments for stealing or cheating on an examination become more sophisticated. Whole careers, after all, are based upon such practices, as the headlines in the newspaper indicate almost any week.

Even in the college years, it is often necessary to repeat: "Yes, there are arguments or justifications for that particular behavior, but you should know that your parents still think that it's wrong and urge you not to do it." In political language that is called "drawing the line." It should be done not to end a discussion but to make it clear where parents stand. In religious history, the life of St. Thomas More dramatizes the necessity of having to do that once in a while when all else fails.

RACISM

In the family, racism raises its head before the child goes to school. The ugly epithets *kike* or *nigger* or *wop* have all the fascination of other forbidden words, and if they are not used to label someone at the neighborhood playground, they are used in sayings or stories, repeated quizzically or enthusiastically by young children. At that time, it is easy to say that such talk is offensive to a friend and therefore should not be repeated. But admonitions of this kind probably make little impression if they are not accompanied by reading and discussion. Elementary books about children of other lands and stories and films about the plight of people persecuted for their beliefs help children identify with others brought up in environments different from their own.

How could anyone ever regard migrant workers' children scornfully, for example, after hearing Cesar Chavez' story of traveling from farm to farm and from school to school during the 1930s and seeing his father refused service at a roadside diner simply because he was Mexican? Young children who become impatient at a parent's lecturing on the evils of discrimination take in these stories with a full appreciation of the personal suffering that they dramatize. Television documentaries and specials, even ones that I found less than convincing myself, left a deep impression on two of my daughters, who could not define antisemitism but who knew from stories of the Holocaust that it is an evil to be resisted.

I am still not sure how to proceed with older children, although I think that their friendships with contemporaries of different racial backgrounds are crucial. Even in college, however, the jokes about black people are current, I have been sorry to learn, and students with strong personal associations sometimes fail to make the connection between their affection for people and their tolerance of practices that are basically racist. What can parents say in the face of such prejudice, except to name it, and hope that the message will carry some weight in future behavior? In addition, parents must support church, social, and advocacy groups that work systematically to combat racist policies.

Racism, that is, the exclusion or mistreatment of people because of their ancestry, culture, religion, race, or language, has plagued human beings for centuries, as one knows from the Old Testament. So much a part of Western culture, so deep and subtle at times, it is a difficult injustice to confront directly. Even the churches have been reluctant to identify and hesitant to eradicate it, as Martin

Luther King, Jr. pointed out 20 years ago: "In the midst of blatant injustices inflicted upon the Negro," he wrote in *Letter from Birmingham Jail,* "I have watched churchmen stand on the sideline and mouth pious irrelevancies and sanctimonious trivialities. In the midst of a mighty struggle to rid our nation of racial and economic injustice, I have heard many ministers say: 'Those are social issues, with which the Gospel has no real concern!' "

For middle-class families, racism becomes invisible when people of other cultures are systematically excluded from the world they inhabit—their churches, schools, colleges, clubs, and industries. Deprived of these basic rights—as defined by recent Catholic teachings, at least—blacks were thus denied any real representation in setting up the rules of organizations, agencies, and governments. Others living at the center of an affluent society seldom see, work with, or even notice minorities that are confined to another area of town, attend other schools or churches, or form other communities. In some instances, other races appear only as the objects of jokes.

Many of the causes of racism were addressed directly by the civil-rights movement during the late 1950s and 1960s, and considerable progress was made in some areas of the country to address the grievances of people long subjected to discrimination. Yet, as Martin Luther King, Jr. pointed out shortly before his death in 1968, the civil-rights movement was only part of a larger movement addressing violence and injustice against people, two aspects of the same system. Such a movement—and Catholic social teachings stressed this point later—has a major goal: the re-structuring of a society by nonviolent means.

SEXISM

The family is the first place where patterns of behavior are established and, therefore, the first place where all the stereotypes imposed upon men and women by the wider culture are faced. In the home, parents can at least clear a space in which children see other, less discriminatory behavior between the sexes, where fathers take responsibility for household chores and mothers pursue public careers. In this, as in much of the education for peace and justice, it is the manner in which parents speak with and treat one another that shapes the values of the children.

Beyond that, parents must make a conscious effort to see that all children are given equal responsibility in family activities, in sports, and other school activities. Language and behavior that discriminate against boys or girls must be addressed in the home, so that children might resist such patterns still common in the schools and on the playground. Boys must be as free as girls to be sensitive and courteous; girls must be as free as boys to be assertive and strong-minded.

The subjugation of women in our culture takes many forms, most effectively dramatized for me the afternoon my oldest daughter came home from a "career day" in her high school. The administration had outlined for her various career choices, all circumscribed by and tailored to what they defined as "women's work." Had she chosen any one of them, I would have supported her, but the fact that nursing and secretarial jobs were presented as the only options made me very angry indeed. As an intelligent, resourceful, and able person, she should have been encouraged to follow any vocation that her ability and capacity for hard work suited her for. But already in high school she was being channeled and in a very real sense discriminated against.

This experience led me to pay closer attention to the whole debate over the Equal Rights Amendment and to listen more carefully to the justifiable complaints of my female contemporaries. In the alumnae magazine of my wife's college, I read, for example, about a scholar and president of one of the country's leading institutions of learning who was told that she was probably admitted to Yale University graduate school because she was less attractive than other women applicants and therefore less likely to marry before completing her degree.

In subsequent discussions and reading, I came to understand how and why such injustices imprison men as well as women. It is no easy task to right these wrongs, particularly since some writings on the subject have been as mean-spirited as the tracts supporting a male-dominated culture. But the changes made possible through the women's movement are truly liberating for all. At its best, the women's movement advocates not only treating women as equals, but also seeing how valuable are the duties that they have traditionally assumed, such as the care of children, the special care and education of others, and so on. An appreciation for the centrality of the development of children leads naturally to a recognition of the importance of human development in many other areas for young and old. The women's movement has been directly responsible for these and so many other insights about the psychology and vulnerability of men and women in contemporary culture.

The family is a crucial place to begin to identify and correct injustices—in language as well as behavior—that the feminist movement brings to public attention. It is a place where people can learn to "fight fairly" in identifying and addressing grievances between the sexes among people manipulated by the social system.

The right to be angry and the recognition of the importance of conflict in human relationships are especially crucial to altering ways of speaking and acting on these issues in the home, beginning with the relationship between husband and wife and moving to the rest of the family. Children may come to understand the fact that love and conflict are not mutually exclusive. Since conflict is inevitable, not only with other people but also within one's self (as a person grows older, develops new interests, and takes on new responsibilities), parents are wise to address it, bringing in outside help if necessary.

Jean Baker Miller, a psychiatrist, said that in the past "for a woman to feel conflict with men has meant that something is wrong with her 'psychologically' since one is supposed to 'get along' if one is 'all right.'" She might have said that many men also suffer from a limited view of human relationships and thus fail to speak out even in situations where differing points of view could contribute to better discourse in the public forum as well.

Serious conflicts can sometimes best be aired at occasional (monthly?) family meetings. For less crucial conflicts, such as the division of housework or communal activities, family dinner-table discussions are enough. But even here parents have to make sure that each person has a chance to speak. As in any group of people, the older, verbal ones, male or female, tend to dominate. In the best interests of all, parents must intervene at crucial points and be as explicit as possible about their priorities.

In the early years of our marriage when our children were young my wife and I did very little to address sexism. But as time went on we chose or stumbled onto a few ways of resisting the old stereotypes and of avoiding categorizing the children by sex. Eventually, for example, everyone in the family took a night at the supper dishes, including both parents. Among the younger children, everyone who chooses to play sports is encouraged and supported. For the youngest girl, the opportunities for playing basketball and softball were particularly liberating, since she loves them as much as any of her brothers do. Even here I had to make a special point of going to her games (or avoiding them) as conscientiously as I did the boys'.

Men, by their place in the social structure, contribute to the injustice of the status quo often without knowing it. For many people, these injustices have only recently become apparent. I was unaware, for example, of the discrimination against women in higher education until I was directly involved in accompanying a woman in a male-dominated institution through interviews and the initial stages of hiring. Had anyone told me beforehand about the kind of remarks made to her—an experienced, intelligent, and accomplished scholar—I would not have believed them. Men I knew to be sensitive, thoughtful, and insightful on a whole range of issues referred to her as a "busy little girl" or made ridiculous, nearly slanderous remarks about her, something they had never done in reference to male candidates for the same position. What kind of an educational environment, I kept thinking, is that for young women, including my own daughters and nieces, to grow into?

Discrimination against women is often symbolized and perpetuated by language and by the literature young children read. Therefore, it is important to make necessary changes in expressions that exclude women and to recommend readings by and about women from the time children are very young. Parents also have to make a special effort to see that the boys in the family are not senselessly channeled into narrowly defined male roles or denied the chance to develop skills in areas traditionally limited to females. This is one area in which the schools have been helpful, in curriculum changes and revised textbooks, but in the church, women are still treated as second-class citizens.

Altering the language of liturgy and religious discussion is therefore especially significant and can begin at home. Making that change is sometimes a simple matter, and young people are often sensitized quickly and easily. My daughter returned from her first year in a Catholic women's college with this pointed revision of a traditional prayer: "In the name of the Mother and the Daughter and the Holy Spirit. Awoman."

Other useful recommendations on vacuuming the dustier corners of religious language have been proposed by clergy and laity. "He who believes and is baptized will be saved" might be revised to read "Whoever believes and is baptized shall be saved"; "Family of Man" to "The Human Family"; "Forefathers" to "Ancestors," and so on. Many of these changes help to clarify thought and to enhance the quality of the language, grown careless in its frequent and misleading references to the male gender only. Alma Trinor, a feminist and lexicographer, makes the same point in arguing that the word "man" in its extended senses "is the most overworked noun in the language and most definitely excludes women no matter what dictionaries say to the contrary." Pointing this out to children in a casual comment helps to acquaint them with the larger issues.

In addition to the usual arguments against restricting women to subservient, second-class citizenship in the social order and to being confined figuratively to the back of the bus, there is a particular problem in the Catholic Church. Women still face the blank wall of historical precedent in their efforts to be treated as mature human beings in the church. And in spite of their intelligence and leadership ability, they are persistently passed over simply because they are female.

Parents can address this particular problem in the family by stressing the contributions of women in religious history. Special attention needs to be given not only to the lives of the saints but also to the history of women religious in their devotion to peace and justice, particularly in their ministry to the poor. Since Vatican II, women religious have been among the most articulate and courageous activists in addressing the injustices of contemporary culture.

In the home, it is important to make a conscious effort to stress stories, films, and histories in which women play central roles. The more natural this appears to young children, in their own surroundings, the more likely they are to make those values a part of their lives. Public programs in the parish and school can make the point that women not be forced to occupy the usual roles as secretary and head of the refreshment committee. These may seem minor points in dealing with sexism, but they are means,

JUSTICE

like that of clearing up discriminatory language, of building a more just society.

"Since women are becoming ever more conscious of their human dignity, they will not tolerate being treated as mere material instruments, but demand rights befitting a human person both in domestic and public life," John XXIII said in 1960. But that statement, in *Pacem in Terris,* giving a positive view of the women's movement, has not been evident in recent papal statements. Increasingly, however, some American bishops, priests, and theologians have begun to recognize what many religious people have maintained for a long time: Sexism is one of the major impediments to a just religious institution.

The absence of women in primary administrative and celebratory roles deprives the church of the richness and diversity of the faithful at a time when it needs the best minds and sensibilities to respond to the global community. Where women have assumed leadership positions in campus, rural, and urban ministries, the result is a broader awareness and diversity in understanding the Gospel.

In my area of the country, women have been the most powerful messengers of the social teachings, extending the ministry of the Word into areas of the city that might never have been reached by the male clergy. From one layman's point of view at least, the continued exclusion of women from a central place in ministry is an unnecessary limitation and hampering of the power of the Word. It amounts to a violation of faith as well as of justice. Through parish councils and diocesan organizations, clergy and laity must insist that girls and women occupy central places in religious celebration, education, and administration. Parents need to know that the expectations established at home are fulfilled outside the family, with models available to them in all areas of the institutional church.

POVERTY AND HUNGER

Peace and justice are not "new" principles "tacked on" to religion. They are essential to the functioning of the family, both individually and collectively. A renewed emphasis on them through the teachings of the church amounts to a rediscovery or a refounding of the family on which the future of human history depends. Unless an appreciation for the interdependence of peoples in the global family permeates the consciousness of the human race, recent encyclicals and pastoral letters suggest there may be no future parents or children.

In its wisdom, the church points toward social justice in an effort not only to alter the priorities of the world but also to alter the priorities of the church in favor of more personal, individualistic concerns. As the first experience of society or community, the family is the obvious place for learning, testing, and maintaining a commitment to people living in poverty and hunger, as well as others neglected or ignored by larger social and economic structures.

"We wish to personify the Christ of a poor and hungry people," Paul VI said to the people of Latin America in 1968. In such statements, recent popes recognize the fact that poverty and hunger are the permanent agonies of the wretched of the earth, those people who make up what Michael Harrington calls "the vast majority." They are the 750 million people who earn less than $75 a year, who cannot read this book because they are illiterate, and who cannot buy it because it would cost them a month's supply of food.

Details of this kind may be simply too overwhelming for children—as they are for grown-ups—and it will do parents little good to impose such information on them without relating it to their own lives and experiences. Yet parents can make these truths part of the religious education of their children by linking them to the other justice issues and by suggesting wherever possible the relationship between hunger and the arms race, poverty, and racism, both locally and internationally. Parents remind their children in order to remind themselves so that the poor do not become invisible.

This is particularly necessary in the 1980s, a decade when the government and the people of the U.S. appear to be turning their backs on "the wretched of the earth," as Michael Harrington calls the billion people who live "a daily agony" of poverty and hunger. Is it coincidental that this government and people began to turn their backs on the poor of their own country shortly after they turned their backs on the poor of the world?

Yet there are remedies to world hunger as citizens' groups, such as Bread for the World, have indicated. Increased production of food alone will not solve the problem, but altering the priorities, such as guaranteeing the right of food to every citizen, could do so. Impressing upon children the right of every person to life, to food, and to liberty is a beginning of this process.

Bread for the World recommends fundamental changes that could be brought about through the following policies: (1) reforming United States' assistance abroad, with the separation of development assistance from military assistance (separating appropriations for guns to the governments of Third World nations, for example, and food for their people); (2) controlling multinational corporations and agribusinesses (regulating the unregulated behavior of big business in its use of land, people, and resources); (3) reducing military spending.

An understanding of hunger provides one of the clearest, most immediate, and obvious reference points for other justice issues. The theologian Dorothee Solle made the point that although we cannot be hungry for the poor, "it is possible to share their hunger for justice." People need this hunger to grow, too, she added, "and we cannot wash away the blood of the guiltless poor in blaming nature, the drought, overpopulation, and underdevelopment."

Families must remain conscious of the difficulty that most people of the world face in winning the barest sustenance from the soil. Growing even a small garden or, if necessary, a few plants inside the house can help children appreciate the delicate balance between nature and human beings and how easily the whole system can be undone by careless treatment of the earth. Such activities, when the children are very young, help to encourage a sense of wonder and realism about the gift of food.

Our friends have been more influential at times in promoting justice than my wife and I have, and their effect on our children is a telling lesson on the importance of community in developing that "new awareness" spoken of in the encyclicals. The most obvious example in our family has been the influence of several young men and women about ten years older than our children, people of college age in the 1960s and 1970s, who helped to initiate the local

Catholic Worker House and to sustain other peace activities after the media lost interest in movements for social change.

In almost any conversation in which the foolishness of altruism or a complaint about "those people on welfare" is mentioned around our children, one of them is likely to refer to a young student they used to play football with who still devotes much of his time to feeding the hungry of the city. An all-around person in their minds inevitably works for peace and justice because their friend fixed that in their sensibilities more immediately than their parents did. "When I read Ayn Rand in class and people started agreeing with her philosophy about not sacrificing yourself for others, I told them about Frank and his feeding and clothing people at the Mustard Seed," my son said recently, "and I thought he dealt with that issue better than Rand did."

As a person whose idea of roughing it is a motel without air conditioning, however, I find it difficult to bring myself to think and, even more, to act upon what I know to be true here. But my children have helped me realize the implications of poor nutrition and irresponsible health practices. In this instance, they have done better at promoting justice than I have. My attitude has always been, as a friend put it in speaking about the three goals of the Catholic Worker movement: cult (liturgy), culture (literature), and cultivation (farming), "I am all for cult and culture; the cultivation will have to be done by somebody else." If my children can get me eventually to work in the garden that they established, I will know the revolution has been accomplished.

In the meantime, I am trying to learn more about the

interrelationships between diet, agribusiness, and world hunger. Organizations such as Bread for the World and Oxfam-America have been particularly helpful in this education. So has a local campaign, through the Coalition for Peace and Justice, a diocesan group working on hunger and violence. In her excellent book of recipes and in various other commentaries Frances Moore Lappé says finding nutritionally-sound alternatives to our present diet in the United States will not solve the world's hunger problems. "But establishing a sense of our direct impact on the earth through food" is an important step in changing our cultural patterns of waste.

In recent years, in the work of the United Nations and in Catholic social teachings, there is a general recognition that peace and justice—and indeed the survival of the planet—depends upon a restructuring of the production and distribution of the world's food. The 1975 U.N. document on *The New International Economic Order,* supported by 77 nations, calls attention to this fact and establishes general guidelines for sharing the world's wealth. In the coming years, the U.S. will work to either strengthen or weaken such proposals. With recent social encyclicals as a guide, through awareness and action, American families can help move these proposals along.

OTHER ECONOMIC AND POLITICAL ISSUES

The tensions parents face in trying to teach social justice to their children are ones they need to try to understand themselves along the way, because children will face the tensions too, if they take on the parents' values. They are the tensions that come of being critical of the status quo and of American political and economic structures while living in the midst of them; of being in conflict with our friends and neighbors who seldom question those structures while working with them from day to day; of having to say "No" to what our friends believe in, but in loving and caring for them along the way.

And the more one works to follow the teachings of the church on peace and justice, the more one is likely to rec ognize and challenge the almost religious fervor of American capitalism, the one dominant faith of our culture. Although, as one Canadian bishop put it, on this continent capitalism has "a civilized face," it appears as anything but civilized to the rest of the world. And John Paul II, in *Laborem Exercens*, criticized what he called the abuses of "rigid capitalism," which frequently places profit above the well-being of the worker.

At this point, parents are tempted to draw back, thinking, "My family and I can live a just life without addressing these other economic issues because they are something different." How much I wish this were true, but it just isn't. For a full understanding of the issues linking all people of the global parish, one must plunge into deeper waters.

Although parental commitment to justice makes it difficult for children in the early years, as they grow older they begin to see relationships and to make connections themselves. Even when they don't agree with a parent's value judgment, they do understand it and, depending upon their sophistication, they sometimes support the logic of social justice by their own insights and evidence. At this point, children are ready for further education on the interrelationships between peace and justice, and they may push parents to do some more homework of their own.

In their high-school and college classes in accounting and history and economics, children—even in Catholic schools—may not hear about the fact that the profit the investor makes often comes from the company's failure to pay workers a decent wage. And the fact that some people have two homes and three cars and most people have none may never present itself as a serious ethical dilemma in their philosophy or religion courses. "But then," a parent may be thinking, "I haven't even resolved those conflicts in my own mind."

POLITICAL OPPRESSION

An element of frankness is important in the thinking, talking, and resisting of injustice in and through the family. It may help in clarifying these conflicts if families make use not of name-calling or blaming, but of frankness, in order to understand things for what they are. Much of the confusion in trying to teach values is directly related to the failure to name injustices. That reluctance occurs because much of the language drummed into American ears is meant to confuse rather than to clarify issues. In recent history, for example, words such as *exploitation, imperialism, manipulation,* and *domination* have been practically expunged from everyday usage, as if they did not apply to what happens to people in an economic system in which profit is the prime motive.

Because of its economic and military power, the U.S. has both a direct and indirect effect on the behavior of some foreign governments toward their own people. Too often the alliance between American business interests and repressive national governments has resulted in the systematic repression of Third World peoples. Even instruments of torture are manufactured and sold by American companies, as was the case in Southeast Asia, with foreign police learning their trade in American police academies. Such economic and political repression, according to Noam Chomsky, is "functionally related to the needs of the U.S. . . . helping to stifle unions and contain reformist threats that might interfere with business's freedom of action. The proof of the pudding is that U.S. bankers and industrialists have consistently welcomed the 'stability' of the new client fascist order, whose governments [are] savage in their treatment of dissidents, priests, labor leaders, peasant organizers, and others who threaten 'order'." And ignorance of what goes on, in America's name, is often the result of the complicity of forces responsible for injustices and violence abroad and the suppression or manipulation of information at home.

The American bishops have consistently spoken out against these injustices and in support of the United Nations Universal Declaration of Human Rights, which denounces manipulation of smaller nations by the larger ones. Both in 1975 and later during the bicentennial year, they addressed themselves to this topic, stating that "internationally, the pervasive presence of American power creates a responsibility to use that power in the service of human rights."

Political repression, that is, depriving persons of their rights of citizenship, is usually associated with dictatorships or police states, but it is a common practice in so-called democratic countries as well: those guardians of the great liberal traditions, freedom of speech, press, and assembly. The most obvious victims of political repression in the United States have been Native Americans and other minorities, who have suffered at the hands of the white majority throughout our history.

People who were "different" have been silenced in subtle and not so subtle ways for their beliefs and practices, and it is important that young people know this history so that it is not repeated. In the 17th century, Mary Dyer, whose statue stands near the Massachusetts Statehouse, was executed because of her beliefs and practices as a Quaker; in 1919, Emma Goldman, Alexander Berkman, and over 200 other people were deported to France because of their unpopular opinions. A declaration of war against Germany in 1917 brought harassment and persecution to many German-Americans, similar to that against Japanese-Americans on the West Coast in 1941, and newspapers were suppressed for publishing objections to America's entrance into the First World War.

Political repression has been, in other words, a harsh reality for many in a country that prides itself on constitutional guarantees of speech and assembly. Out of this turmoil, in an effort to protect these rights of citizenship, came the American Civil Liberties Union, which has provided legal representation and aid for people with "unpopular" opinions and ideas. During the Vietnam War, the ACLU assisted many young men who were conscientiously opposed to war, including many Catholics who based their opinions on Catholic social teaching, yet were told, mistakenly, by draft boards that they had no right to do so.

Children and their contemporaries should know that in many communities the ACLU has protected students when freedom of the press for a student newspaper was in jeopardy because of a repressive administrator or unconstitutional ruling by a board of trustees or school committee. And the organization is extremely helpful for families in exploring the rights that represent some of the noblest aspects of English and American history. Limitations on anyone's rights are a threat to the rights of citizenship for all, raising basic and difficult moral questions about privileges and duties under the law.

Political hysteria is always a threat to a good society. In the U.S. during the 1950s, for example, people lost their jobs and even went to prison because they were Communists or because they refused to identify others who had been. During that period, humorously and effectively dramatized in the Woody Allen film "The Witness" (1970) agencies such as the Federal Bureau of Investigation and the Central Intelligence Agency violated the rights of many citizens, opening letters, tapping phone conversations, and circulating hate mail against people critical of the government.

Many American citizens fiercely critical of similar practices in foreign countries said nothing against such repressive tactics at home. They failed to make the necessary connection between economic exploitation abroad and political repression at home and so helped to make the 1950s one of the darkest periods in American history, with the rise and dominance of the military bureaucracy.

For the poor and for black people, the consequences of political repression are even more serious, since they extend not only to the denial of equal rights, but also to the denial of legal representation and, occasionally, to death. For this reason, organizations such as Amnesty International as well as various Catholic organizations actively work against the death penalty, which is frequently used as a means of punishing racial, ethnic, and religious groups, particularly in Latin America.

UNEMPLOYMENT AND UNJUST WAGES

For people born and brought up in the U.S. since World War II, the consequences of economic injustice—poverty and unemployment—sometimes seem very abstract. With only vague impressions of the Great Depression, Americans have not known the deprivation that a previous generation experienced when, in 1933, 25 percent of the labor force was out of work. Even people who were poor while in school or when their children were very young have never known what it means to be completely destitute, with no one to lean on in emergencies for money or food or clothing.

All the time my family and I were living on $225 a month while I was in graduate school we still knew we would never starve. We could always phone our families (collect) in a crisis for a gift or a care package to get us through. Usually we looked forward to or perhaps at least dreamed of a better future. By the late 1970s, as jobs disappeared and inflation increased, we might still have moved to another section of the United States where opportunities for employment were better.

Many of those cushions disappeared in recent years for young and old alike, and for the first time in 50 years, high-school and college graduates had nothing to look forward to but odd jobs at low pay. Even at this time, however, the distance between the typical middle-class American and the average person in the rest of the world is very great, in terms of food, clothing, shelter, and employment. Here again recent papal encyclicals, including Paul VI's "On the Development of Peoples" and "A Call to Action: Letter on the 80th Anniversary of *Rerum*

Novarum" were among the most perceptive statements of the state of affairs for the poor everywhere.

The earlier writings of the popes and the bishops and the experience of working people are important to remember. From the time of Leo XIII, in the late 19th century, the church began to set down conditions for wages, working conditions, and benefits, and that tradition helps families appreciate workers' struggles to organize in new industrial areas of this country and abroad.

With the publication of Pius XI's encyclical *Quadragesimo Anno* on the 40th anniversary of *Rerum Novarum,* Catholic social teachings turned increasingly to the rights of workers. Each time, the popes expanded on the concerns associated with St. Thomas Aquinas's definition of justice as "the strong and firm will to give each their due." This definition, applied initially to the relationship between worker and entrepreneur, helped to sustain the argument that workers deserved payment because it was good for industry, the general economy, and the social order.

But since World War II, in a world of privileged nations and peoples, the focus in Catholic social teachings shifted from the transactions between worker and owner to the nature and basic rights of human beings. John Paul II's *Laborem Exercens,* on the 90th anniversary of *Rerum Novarum,* further emphasized "the principle of the priority of labor over capital," saying that "work constitutes a foundation for the formation of family life, which is the natural right" to which human beings are called. Unjust wages and working conditions, therefore, are a threat to family life. And parents are wise to point out to children the achievements of the labor movement in bringing about decent working conditions.

In recent years, the United Farm Workers and others not covered by labor legislation of the 1930s dramatized the plight of the worker in the South and West, with support from the American bishops. In principle, if not always in its own labor and hiring practices, the church has indicated its continued resistance to economic and political injustice. But like any other principle, that commitment is not visible until people apply it, test it, and sustain it through their own words and actions.

A commitment to social justice is not a decision that people make and then forget. It is, as the literature and songs from all movements for social change admit, a continuing struggle. Parents try to keep the history of struggles for justice alive through their own example, in suggestions for children's education, and through some of the people they meet and spend their time with. For most of the world's people, families have to remind themselves, the struggle for economic and political justice is only beginning.

4

Peace

"Peace is not merely the absence of war. Nor can it be reduced solely to the maintenance of a balance of power between enemies. Nor is it brought about by dictatorship. Instead, it is rightly and appropriately called 'an enterprise of justice' (Isaiah 32:7)."

Gaudium et Spes (78)

The late General Omar Bradley put the matter bluntly. "We know more about war than we do about peace—more about killing than we know about living." In a world almost continually at war since 1914, is it any wonder that children grow up with more knowledge about guns, bombers, and war than they do about citizenship, reconciliation, and nonviolent movements for social change? And they will not learn about the latter concepts and their history unless parents make a point of teaching them from the time they are very young.

It is certainly better to raise questions about violence and aggression than to suppress them, since for most children in American culture they are natural impulses or at least natural responses to what they see around them. They are also common themes in literature of the Western world: in fairy tales and Greek drama, in the plays of Shakespeare and the stories of Flannery O'Connor. Allowing children to recognize these powerful impulses in human nature is an important part of learning and of their growing up.

There is no best way of addressing violence and aggression, but they must not be ignored.

Margaret Drabble has written a powerful short story about a mother who saved for months to buy her child a play gun for his birthday. She did this out of love, not out of a wish to encourage violence. When, after months of preparation and much adversity she finally made her way to the department store to buy it, however, her "victory" was spoiled by a self-righteous young demonstrator who shamed the mother in front of everyone.

"Instead of simply condemning violence we should think very seriously about it from an early age on," the psychologist Bruno Bettelheim says, "and all through life: about what causes violence in ourselves and in others; what could be done to prevent these causes from occurring, or from resulting in violent actions; how energy aroused by stimuli which evoke violent feelings could be channeled into constructive behavior."

One of the saddest developments in contemporary American life is the tendency to regard warmaking as the only way of channeling these impulses. Before World War II, the military forces generally took second place to more basic concerns of the American people, and such practices as the singing of "The Star Spangled Banner" and trooping to the colors (or placing a flag in church sanctuaries) were restricted to special occasions. They were not, as they are now, the preliminary ceremonies for almost every public occasion, from college football games to performances of the Boston Symphony Orchestra.

Love of one's native country is noble and just, particularly if it leads to humane policies toward all citizens. But uncritical or militant patriotism can lead to chauvinism and eventually to hostility toward different cultures.

Some of the worst villainies against humanity have been justified by one country or region assuming itself superior to another, and church teaching rightly directs attention toward the equality and rights of all peoples. The mottoes of the great American apostles of nonviolence, from Thomas Paine and William Lloyd Garrison to the present, support this principle: "My country is the world; my countrymen are all mankind," for example, appeared on the masthead of Garrison's newspaper, the *Liberator*, in the mid-19th century.

Militarism arises in various ways in the family, and parents are wise to try to answer as carefully as possible such questions as "But aren't the Russians determined to dominate us?" and "Aren't they the real cause of the arms race and, through Castro, of the peasants' revolt in Central America?" These questions are too important to be treated lightly, for the rationale supporting them is pervasive in schools and colleges, and any objective discussion of them is rare in popular newspapers, public speeches, and conservative religious circles.

How much parents go into such matters depends, as always, on the age and interest of the child, but a satiric comment or a sarcastic remark about an opponent's point of view is not sufficient. Misinformation must be addressed directly, particularly with peace principles, where children will very likely be required to justify their opinions before classmates, teachers, or even public officials. Remaining courteous but firm in discussing such highly charged issues is also useful training for young people who will face similar conflicts in many other areas of their lives.

The competition between the U.S.S.R. and the United States, for example, can be put into the proper perspective. A look at a map of American military bases around the world will suggest why foreign countries are justifiably fearful of American militarism, including its use of the atomic bomb (the only country ever to do so) during World War II. Is there any restraint once a militarist government gets the upper hand, one wonders, remembering the destruction of Dresden, Hiroshima, and Nagasaki?

It is important, too, to make the point that most arguments supporting the arms race and undercutting co-existence with the U.S.S.R. do not adequately take into account the Russian people's long history as victims of aggression and their present concern about the forces ranged around them. Even the undeniably aggressive actions of the present Soviet regime have to be seen in the light of that history and the justifiable fears that resulted. Germany's destruction of Soviet land is still evident to anyone visiting that country, giving the Russians an understanding of the threat of total war unknown to most Americans. In any case, whatever criticisms we have of the U.S.S.R., the arms race can only make matters worse and threatens us all with oblivion.

But the most important question to raise in family discussions of the threatening confrontation between the U.S. and the U.S.S.R. is not who is right and who is wrong. The question is how to defuse an explosive, no-win situation and to cultivate ways of thinking that will counteract the military mentality.

The appeal of militarism remains very strong among young people, and the sales pitch of the Army, Navy, and Air Force recruiters and ROTC programs that offer scholarship aid during hard times are understandably attractive to students. They need to consider carefully their choices and the consequences of them.

It goes without saying that parents must stick by their children even when the children make choices directly contrary to their own values. They must know that they can change their minds without loss of love or respect. Parents must remain open to them, in spite of fundamental disagreements. Thinking aloud is one of the best ways to clarify thoughts, particularly as children get older. And change and development are essential to parents as well as to children.

Beyond that, parents wishing to uphold church teachings on peace and justice need to alert children to the dangers of militarism, as of racism and sexism, and to recommend the power of nonviolence in American history. In schools and religious education, they must challenge the common practice of associating social change with violence, particularly in a country which has a long tradition of nonviolent movements toward independence, abolitionism, women's liberation, workers' rights, and peace.

Many histories of this country focus exclusively on military battles, giving the impression that all was won by violence, rather than by day-to-day struggles of people building a just society nonviolently. Even the movement for independence is taught as if it were accomplished by General Washington's taking command of the colonial army, without reference to Paine's *Common Sense,* nonviolent actions against colonial governors, Samuel Adams's Committee of Correspondence, or farmers' revolts in North Carolina. Similarly, the antislave movement, in the work of William Lloyd Garrison. Stephen Symonds Foster, and the Grimke sisters, before 1860, may have liberated more people than the violent and humiliating war against the South.

Violent conflict is not always avoidable and it sometimes gets results; even Gandhi said that in the face of injustice, violent resistance is better than doing nothing. But the better thing is to make the opponent one's friend. Martin Luther King, Jr. listed four basic steps to any successful settlement of a violent confrontation, and his recommendations are useful for parents settling a dispute at the neighborhood ballpark as well as for citizens resisting the Pentagon and the MX missile. They are: collection of the facts to determine whether injustice exists; negotiation; self-purification, and direct action.

Each step toward the settlement of violent or potentially violent disputes is important, and anyone knowledgeable about movements for social change has seen these principles in action. As a teacher in a black college in North Carolina in the early days of picketing, sit-ins, and freedom rides, I saw young black men and women in a potentially violent setting maintain discipline and commitment in many confrontations. That campaign still has much to teach by philosophy and example. Can people put their trust in any other means of social change?

The story of how the United States came to put its trust in war and violence is long and complex, giving a valuable perspective on the present. Part of it was of our own making; part of it was an inheritance from colonial Europe; and part of it was a historical accident.

All through American history, however, there have been men and women who understood and resisted the destructive forces that presently threaten to overwhelm us. They said long ago what many of us are only now beginning to understand about large standing armies and nationalistic propaganda. Eugene Victor Debs, Indiana labor organizer and draft resister, said of the First World War: "I do not believe that the shedding of blood bears any actual testimony to patriotism.... On the contrary, I believe that warfare, in all of its forms, is an impeachment of our social order, and a rebuke to our much vaunted Christian civilization."

Although heroes of nonviolence are given much less attention in secular and even religious education than those of violent battles, some recent books and films tell the story of people such as John Woolman (1720–72), the first draft resister; Abigail Kelley Foster (1811–87), tax resister; Emma Goldman (1869–1940), feminist and labor agitator; Martin Luther King, Jr. (1929–68); and Dorothy Day (1897–1980). Their biographies provide suitable stories for children because the stories are fascinating and inspiring and closer to the values espoused by the church than those commonly cited.

What I am suggesting is that the recent teachings of the church on social justice are in keeping with the nobler aspects of American tradition and that parents would do well to build on that past, to encourage their children to love their native land. Too often, I think, Catholics regard their social teachings as being in conflict, somehow, with American history. For years, immigrants to the United States thought the best way to prove their patriotism was to die, rather than to live for their adopted country.

Children should be taught about the bravery and loyalty of their ancestors in confronting injustice and learn that there are better ways to prove a person's courage and dedication than preparing for war. Through the traditional teachings related to the just war theory and recent encyclicals, Christians can address the root causes of violence. The manufacture of arms in this country and their distribution to poorer countries deprive people of basic resources—food, homes, education—by squandering them on products that are economically valueless. The Vatican II document, *Gaudium et Spes,* "The Pastoral Constitution on the Church in the Modern World," called attention to this form of injustice saying that "the arms race is an utterly treacherous trap for humanity, and one which injures the poor to an intolerable degree."

The tradition for counseling peace rather than war was established centuries ago in the words of Moses: "I have set before you life and death, the blessing and the curse. Choose life, then, that you and your descendants may live" (Deut. 30:19).

THE DRAFT

The draft, or conscription, is only one aspect of militarism, yet it is the issue that, besides war taxes, imposes itself most directly on American families. From a very early age, boys are likely to think about where they stand in relationship to the armed forces, and recent history seems to say to them that fighting a war, rather than living in peace, is the expected manner of conducting themselves in the world.

From 1940 to 1973 young men coming of age faced conscription automatically. At no previous period in American history was a peacetime draft tolerated by the general populace, so that a popular bumper sticker saying that "The draft is an un-American activity" is at least historically accurate. In 1973, through the efforts and personal sacrifices of thousands of young draft resisters and older men and women active in counseling and repeal, the draft was put on a stand-by status. The ultra-resistance, beginning with the draft board raids by Daniel and Philip Berrigan and Thomas and Marjory Melville in 1968, had significantly impeded the function of the selective service system and strengthened the movement for repeal during the Vietnam War. Then, after seven years, in 1980, registration for the draft was revived, with the threat of induction looming on the horizon.

Since the 18th century and particularly since World War I, there has been a strong tradition of draft resistance in the United States, and in late 1981 almost half the citizenry opposed revival of conscription. Since 1933, there has been a consistent resistance among Catholics, growing first out of the Catholic Worker movement and, shortly afterward, the Association of Catholic Conscientious Objectors, the first corporate Catholic witness against war. The history of the ACCO, told with considerable wit and telling anecdotes by Gordon Zahn, shows it as "the essential link between the Catholic peace witness of World War II and the more extensive Catholic resistance to the war in Vietnam."

As a draft counselor and as a father, I feel strongly that young people should be allowed to make a choice about how they deal with the draft, without undue pressure from anyone. It is a serious decision—one that is rightly described as a matter of life and death, carrying serious moral, social, and political implications. Good counseling is crucial, so that the young people learn as much as they can about draft laws and regulations.

In many communities, local diocesan offices of Catholic Charities or the Council of Churches provide draft counseling or put a parent in touch with trained draft counselors. In my city, the Interfaith Center for Draft Information, founded in 1969, has been an effective agency of cooperation among Catholic, Protestant, and Jewish congregations and a model for similar programs in other areas.

What to do about draft registration is one of the major decisions faced by a person in late adolescence, at a time when the urge to rebel against parents—to assert identity—is strongest. It is a time when rebellion seems to the young person to be the better part of valor. For this reason, too, an informed draft counselor—a person whom parents know to be considerate and open—is invaluable.

Now that the prospect of a new draft is increasing, the need for well-informed draft counselors is again evident. In registering, as in facing induction, young people must be careful to document their choices, particularly if they seek an exemption or wish to establish a claim as conscientious objectors. They are wise to keep records, including documentation of any public expression of their beliefs. In some dioceses they can file a copy of their intention by sending a letter to the bishop. They may wish to write also to the Central Committee of Conscientious Objectors, listed in the resources section.

Recent statements by the American bishops on registration and the draft are useful in forming consciences and in aiding parents to help registrants reach a decision. In spite of wide-scale opposition to the draft, in the American past and in recent times, it refuses to go away. As a country deeply mired in militarism, the prospect of conscription will undoubtedly face parents and children for years to come.

Having spoken about the importance of counseling—

that is, of a nonjudgmental aid to decision making on the issue of conscription—I must now speak, however, about my own reasons for opposing the draft. I see the draft as a policy that persons committed to peace and justice may wish to resist in every way they can.

My basic objections to the draft are that conscription is not only inequitable and unworkable, but probably unconstitutional as well. My reasons closely resemble those of many Americans, dating from the time of Daniel Webster in the early 19th century, who said that conscription had no place in a society pretending to be democratic.

Resistance to the draft is, in fact, one issue that unites conservatives, such as the late Senator Robert Taft of Ohio and Senator Barry Goldwater of Arizona, and liberals such as Senator Mark Hatfield of Oregon and former senator George McGovern of South Dakota, as well as radicals such as Philip Berrigan and the late Dorothy Day. Opposition is based upon three principal grounds: that conscription infringes unnecessarily on personal freedom, that conscription militarizes the nation, making a declaration of war more likely and more possible; and that, in agreement with a presidential study group known as the Gates Commission in 1970, "conscription induces the military service to use manpower inefficiently."

As a person who has spent hundreds of hours counseling people facing the draft and, more recently, registration, I am aware of the inherent discrimination of compulsory military training. Although people are presumed to know their obligations and rights under the law, neither they, nor the members of the local draft boards, under the old system, did. Many of the boards' mistakes, in fact, not only went uncorrected but also unnoticed by state and national selective service administrations. The price of their mistakes was paid not by the adults in charge but by the young people at their disposal. The directives, bulletins, memos, and regulations concerning medical standards and exemptions are highly technical, sometimes beyond the understanding of the ordinary registrant and the government employees responsible for getting information to the public.

In my experience as a draft counselor, it was not uncommon for boards at the local and even the state level to give wrong information about selective service regulations. School counselors and local lawyers, therefore, depended upon volunteer draft counselors to straighten out the messes made by the so-called official agencies.

Whatever the limitations of the volunteer army, it has at least the merit of being less oppressive and bureaucratic than other alternatives. To those who object, on political grounds, that a volunteer army has trouble attracting recruits, one can only answer, "Yes, of course it does." That is the reason historically that guardians of citizens' rights in this country have insisted that armies be raised on a volunteer basis. In time of emergency, Americans have responded to a voluntary call to arms. Free people will serve when they understand that their freedom is endangered.

Aren't the principles in forming resistance to conscription the ones that a free society must hold? Or do Americans prefer conscripts (as Prussia did, as Hitler's Germany, Stalinist Russia, and other dictatorships did) that are forced to die against their will? Many of our ancestors, particularly those from Central and Southern Europe, came to the United States to avoid conscription. George Wald, Nobel laureate, professor emeritus of biology at

Harvard University and a war resister, said in a rally against draft registration that his father had come to this country for that reason. Young Catholics resisting the draft or making the lawful choice by conscientious objection, therefore, honor not only the noblest teaching of the church and the example of several saints including St. Francis of Assisi, but also historical precedents set by their forebears. They may, in addition, be avoiding an occasion of sin, as Gordon Zahn suggests.

In counseling a child, parents or a draft counselor should provide copies of the statements on the draft by the United States Catholic Conference and the Catholic Peace Fellowship—not in order to push in one direction or the other, but to assist in *making an informed decision about the future.* The parent must respect the individual conscience of the child. Of course it is painful when a child makes a decision directly opposed to the advice of parents. But here, as in many other matters, trust and acceptance of the moral choice made by the child are absolutely essential.

Although the subject of the effects of war and militarism is a large subject, I must mention, in passing, the necessity of not ignoring or dismissing those who enlist in the armed forces, even if we do not agree with them. Many of these young people make that choice without sufficient knowledge and not a few discover that they are conscientious objectors after enlisting, or simply change their minds. I know one young man from a devout family, for example, who first read Tolstoi's religious pamphlets against war and Jim Forest's excellent pamphlet, *Catholics and C.O.,* while he was A.W.O.L., seeking military counseling. The experience of the wounded Vietnam veteran in the popular film, "Coming Home," who denounced American policies in Southeast Asia, was common in the early 1970s. Working for peace includes seeking reconciliation with victims of war, soldiers as well as civilians.

The ravages of war, including its effects on those who survive, are seldom discussed, yet they remain to haunt the participants for the rest of their lives. Resisting war and militarism is one way of trying to keep this circumstance from becoming the common lot of our children as it has been for too many children since 1914.

WAGING PEACE

Commitment to the welfare of the individual person as well as to the global community provides the basis for all church teachings on peace. This effort to preserve the integrity of every person and nation is the focus of attention. From this body of teachings arises the concern for human beings from the first moment of life to its natural conclusion. As Daniel Berrigan, S.J. said of a person's right to life: "Because I believe that all these issues are joined . . . abortion, capital punishment, war . . . integrity compels me to protect life that is endangered. I cannot deny in one situation what I affirm in another."

The serious issues of war and militarism—nuclear submarines, neutron bombs, and conscription—can be overwhelming. Parents presented with such a list of grievances may ask, "What are you trying to do, make me feel guilty?" or "Why should I have to solve problems that I didn't create?" or "It's easy to name injustices, but can't you indicate how to correct them?"

Each of these responses is reasonable, understandable, and to the point. Also, some of the comments in this chapter are theoretical rather than practical. The next chapter, however, includes more suggestions about what a family can do. Before that, I want to address the first two questions I have raised.

First, little is accomplished by self-righteous accusations. It is not only useless and self-serving to impose guilt but also a waste of time. Yes, when pressed to the wall, it feels good to harangue the Secretary of State or the head of a multinational corporation for ignoring the rights of citizens and workers, or the superintendent of schools for not providing draft information for students.

Such exercises in moralism do something for the soul and may keep a person sane when everybody else insists upon being cool and rational in the face of what appear to be insane political judgments. But such behavior does not enable people to change their own lives and thus influence others to do the same. While it is true that some people should feel guilty (and others do, no matter how the issues are presented), the general principle still holds: Alter the structure, rather than attack people, but hold them responsible for their actions at the same time.

The psychological process I am trying to describe is central to social change through nonviolent means, a process people such as Gandhi and Martin Luther King, Jr. understood very well. It is a commitment to speak truth to power and to act. It recognizes also that being right is not as important as waging peace. The desired end is not defeat of the opponent or the imposition of one's ego; it is the reconciliation among all people by seeking the truth.

Second, people *are* responsible for changing things, even when they didn't create the problem. As a citizen of the United States, I have a responsibility to try to influence the policies of my government. I must try to alter the structures that, given our involvement in the affairs of other nations, make hunger, racism, and war almost inevitable. Facing up to my complicity and that of my family—by our silence, if not by our actions—is painful. And guilt may be our first reaction. As people dedicated to nonviolence and reconciliation, however, my family and I must try not to be immobilized by guilt or to impose it on others, but to direct our energies and theirs toward positive change.

Another complication in working for social justice is the tendency to want to do something for others rather than to empower people to do things for themselves. Since this tendency on a national scale has gotten the United States and other imperial powers into positions of manipulation and domination, it may do the same for individuals in a community or in a group.

Since World War II the leadership of this country has often justified its military aid by saying that it was merely trying to help a Third World country. The reality, in Southeast Asia, for example, was that we were attempting to impose our policies through a puppet government. The consequence was a long and brutal war, the deaths of thousands of men, women, and children, the destabilization of the governments of Cambodia and Laos, and the physical destruction of a once rich and beautiful land.

In efforts to learn the truth about justice and peace, a truth to which people with diverse points of view contribute, people will undoubtedly confront some disagreeable facts about themselves as well as their country. But as Flannery O'Connor wrote: "The truth does not change according to our ability to stomach it emotionally . . . and there are long periods in the lives of all of us, and of the saints, when the truth revealed by faith is hideous, emotionally disturbing, downright repulsive."

Such troubled reactions are likely when thinking about the sale of armaments, the subversive operations of the CIA, and U.S. alliances with dictatorships around the world. The truth, in this case, may not make families free, but it may make them more responsible. In the following chapter, I mention a few activities for the family that address these problems at home and in the wider community.

5

But What Can One Family Do?

"Social norms of whatever kind are not only to
be explained but also applied. This is especially
true of the church's teaching on social matters,
which has truth as its guide, justice as its end,
and love as its driving force."

Mater et Magistra

Almost anything seems simpler at times than sorting out
the many questions that present themselves in rearing a
family. And each question inevitably touches many cross-
references, rivalries, and psychological needs among children of different ages, not to mention the financial costs of
food, clothing, shelter, and education. The mere maintenance of the family becomes especially complicated during
times of perennial inflation, which is itself brought on partially by war and military spending.

And people, it seems, even those in the upper ranges of
national income, never talk as if they have enough. This
compulsion for goods, new fashions, automobiles, fancy
foods, and entertainment, contributes to their own and their
children's anxiety, even when they don't wish it to. How
essential it is, then, that parents try to give children a different way of evaluating things and another way of es-
timating their own worth, skills, and usefulness to others.
Over and over parents must uphold, as Jean Baker Miller
says, "the importance of unimportant people" and the value
of participating in the development of others. This chapter

suggests a few ways of doing that, in the home, parish, school, and community.

Being informed about and even sympathetic to movements for social change is a beginning. To act on those sentiments, to put self and family "on the line," is more difficult. This may mean—in addition to building awareness and doing basic education around the family dinner table and through incidents that occur in daily life—writing letters, resisting taxes for armaments, participating in liturgies and public prayer; it may also mean leafleting, picketing institutions associated with injustice, and demonstrating in other ways.

What stimulates young people to action is always a mystery, but one essential factor is the development of their imaginations, so that they will be aware of the pain and joy of other people. Much has been written in this decade about the "me" generation and the culture of narcissism; yet this failure to be concerned with anyone other than oneself is not confined to this generation of young adults. It is a characteristic of people of every age who seem unable "to walk a mile in the moccasins of the other person," as the old saying puts it. How else can people explain not only their behavior toward others, but also their voting for policies that make life harder for the elderly, the poor, the handicapped, the unemployed?

Such insensitivity amounts to a kind of "psychic numbing," in the words of Robert Jay Lifton, whereby people have only a "diminished capacity to feel or inclination to feel" or to take into account the suffering of others. What Professor Lifton found in his research among victims of atomic warfare seems to characterize many people now living under the threat of nuclear weapons. They move toward their own destruction without protest, as governments pile up more bombs and bombers; sometimes they even refuse to give a fair hearing to those still sane enough to warn them of the deadly future programmed by the Pentagon and the war manufacturers.

In order to combat this numbing, parents need to show children that being concerned about others is a natural extension of concern about themselves. This awareness grows out of the most obvious considerations: courtesy, generosity, fairness, even to people with whom they live in disagreement and conflict. In public protests and civil disobedience this manner of behaving is called nonviolence or, in Gandhi's term, *satyagraha,* a Sanskrit word meaning "insistence on truth" or "truth seeking."

Social action is best seen as the work of people who take Catholic social teachings and their responsibilities as citizens seriously. Engaging in such work is one way of teaching children how the American system works.

Parents are wise to consider the strengths and limitations of their own education for political action, about how they did or did not learn to live as free citizens. Seeing my grandmother sort out newspaper clippings on important public issues, setting aside the ones she wished to write her senator and representative about, was crucial to my own education. That said more to me about the value of political action than anything I learned in civics class, making it seem natural and right for "a reasonable person" to spend her time in that manner.

In spite of being proud of their rights of citizenship, many Americans are reluctant to speak publicly. All their basic middle-class reluctance "to make a fool of ourselves" in front of neighbors and friends asserts itself. This is still true, in my own case, at the first thought of speaking out, even for the best of causes. For years, without knowing it, I had assumed that the world could move along somehow, conducting its business, without my taking part in it. That old illusion about living a private life, not bothering myself about congressional votes or the behavior of my elected representatives in local, state, and national governments, died hard. In other words, I understand people's reluctance to move outside their ordinary routines or to subject themselves to time-consuming and frustrating but necessary work for social change.

Having admitted this, I then have to admit that almost every benefit Americans enjoy as workers—from decent pay to health benefits to sick leave—came as a result of people willing to act on their beliefs in justice. I need only to read of the sacrifices of workers in the late 19th and early 20th centuries—many of whom were jailed or fired, because of union organizing—to be reminded of this historical fact. The rights of women, too, are the result of marches, picketing, and fasts by people involved in political agitation then. Rationally, I know that in order to alter the course of events I must take action, but on a rainy Saturday morning, when I am supposed to join a liturgy and rally against the MX missile in front of a local armament manufacturer, it is still hard to leave the house, drive 15 miles, and confront a potentially hostile audience, when I could stay home, read the newspaper, have a second cup of coffee, and loaf.

I think of Dorothy Day, who said that she would not have gotten involved in any public protests, marches, and civil disobedience, if she had not been pushed in to them by Peter Maurin, Ammon Hennacy, Karl Meyer, or other workers. If that is true for that courageous and faithful woman, then I suppose it is not surprising that a similar inertia keeps people from acting on what they know to be true.

For this reason, too, parents must seek out and depend upon a community of people to keep alert, attuned, and persistent. They will encourage us to "make fools of ourselves" when the welfare of others is at stake. The landless, the poor, and the hungry cannot be abandoned; they must remain a permanent part of consciousness, even though the ads on television and magazines pretend that everyone in the world has plenty of money.

Actions are important, too, because only through action does a person become fully conscious of how bad things really are for a large portion of the human race. Only by standing on the street corner, in front of city hall—out where life is lived—are people likely to see the full effects of poverty, hunger, and poor medical care. Only there are people forced to test their grasp of the issues, in speaking to the man or woman on the street who has never talked with anyone before about the draft, nuclear warfare, or gun control.

Difficult as it is at times to walk up to strangers, in house-to-house canvassing, and to hand them a leaflet about conversion to a peace economy, such activity can lead to new perceptions for the canvasser as well as for the other persons. The same is true of debate with an opponent, if a person proceeds without fear of being "wrong"; if discussion goes on to get at the truth and not simply to impose a point of view. That is the purpose of nonviolent action on behalf of peace and justice, from writing letters to Congress to commiting civil disobedience.

FAMILY ACTIVITIES

Some of the work for peace and justice is necessarily done outside the home through community and legislative action. Some of it is determined by local issues, the part of the country or the area of the city in which parents and children live. It may vary depending upon what work they do, what school or parish they attend.

But the home is where parents establish links between justice and peace and their life and activity as a family. They can show that the struggle for peace (to reduce the military budget or support committees against the draft) and the struggle for justice (against racism and sexism) are aspects of the same movement. If this fact is not as evident as it might be, a closer look at the social structure supporting violence and injustice makes it apparent.

There are many jobs that can be done at home to build communities of peace and justice by people with only a small amount of time beyond the daily obligations of work and childrearing. Even a commitment of one hour a week can make a difference not only to a family's awareness, but also to a movement's impact in a community.

During a child's early years and, of course, later on as well, family prayer for justice, incorporated with blessings before meals and special liturgies, contribute to a child's awareness of the needs of others. The crucial factor here is that parents and other older people are present, expressing their own concerns, not merely telling children that they should pray for the hungry, the homeless, the imprisoned. Liturgies celebrating the lives of heroes of nonviolence point up what others have done to help people in need.

A natural development from praying for social justice is setting up a regular program of contributions to a favorite charity or movement group. A container at the center of the table for donations from allowances or paychecks to be sent monthly to the local chapter of Amnesty International or Pax Christi, was one of the more successful means of educating our family when the children were young. Sometimes none of the things parents plan to do accomplish the goals set, and some appeal to one child but not to another. Parents gradually develop a repertory of approaches to get a point across.

Educating children toward appreciation of people of different cultures is more complex. In school, this can sometimes be achieved by setting up a correspondence for your child with a "pen pal" in a foreign country. Here missionary publications are helpful.

The films and materials available through the United Nations, particularly the UNICEF Field Service Department, many of them available through the public library, dramatize the lives of children in other countries. They do so in a manner that enables children to identify with them in an appreciative and respectful way. The films are useful for neighborhood parties or at Halloween as a way of encouraging children and adults to participate in the "trick-or-treat for UNICEF" program, with donations going to buy milk and food for refugee children around the world.

Providing hospitality for visiting workers for the War Resisters League, the United Farm Workers, and Catholic Worker Houses of Hospitality enables children to get to know people who spend every day working for peace and justice. In our experience this had the effect of helping them make a realistic evaluation of the trials and pleasures of that struggle and the faults and virtues of the people involved. It is easy to romanticize or sentimentalize working for social justice if a person has never done it. Talking with activists may dispel any romantic notions about "giving up one's life for the cause"; but it also gives young people a realistic view and appreciation for the dedication and courage it takes to stay on the job day after day. Those associations provided models in several instances for our children as they got older and made decisions about the future.

There are numerous family or community activities that children will contribute to —not always willingly, I should add, but on assignment the first time. Listed below are several that have worked for our family, beginning with the parents but drawing the children into activities that they might not have done otherwise. (Addresses for the organizations mentioned are listed in the back of the book.)

1. Read a paragraph or so from *Year One* at the supper table and send contributions from paychecks or weekly allowances to Jonah House to support the actions at the Pentagon against war, or go to Washington for the annual vigils on the feast of the Holy Innocents, at Christmas time, or during Holy Week.

2. Do an hour of typing or addressing and stuffing envelopes or stapling newsletters (stapling and collating pages will keep a strong 6-year-old busy for at least 30 minutes) for Bread for the World, Pax Christi, Catholic Peace Fellowship, Amnesty International, or similar local groups.

3. Encourage the parish council, the religious education program, or the liturgy committee to address a social justice problem and schedule a talk by a person who is well-

informed on the subject. Six months later, arrange a similar program or liturgy specifically for children.

4. Initiate an annual peace vigil in your town or county seat on Memorial Day with a liturgy in a home or nearby church, on behalf of all victims of war and for a moratorium on nuclear weapons. Provide poster board and magic markers for the children to design and draw their own signs. (Young teenagers will probably balk, but up through age 12 many children will participate.)

5. Send one letter a month to someone who spoke, voted, or acted on behalf of peace and justice. Criticize a representative's vote or compliment him or her for taking a stand. Read the note to the family, ask for and incorporate their comments and suggestions whenever possible, and mail it.

Such activities encourage a reverence for life along the lines suggested by Thomas Berry, S.P., who speaks of the need for a revitalized theology of creation. That theology, he says, should respect the rights of the earth as well as the people on it, including air, water, space, and vegetation. When people dismiss his view as visionary, Berry points out that "corporations, which are not persons, are treated as legal entities, why not trees and rivers? We are much more dependent upon them for life than we are upon corporations!" Such a theology provides a solid base on which to build a perspective from which families might view all life, and an angle of vision, very acceptable to children, that encourages them "to know and to do."

Family activity means integrating, as far as possible, the work of peace and justice in daily life. And people are only beginning to discover how that integration can be done. For this reason families need to be in touch with others in parishes, liturgical groups, centers for peace and justice in a continuing effort for education and action.

In Latin America, the *comunidades de base* are important in turning both the church and the larger society toward the needs of the poor and the oppressed. In the U.S., such communities undoubtedly take other forms, given the cultural and historical differences, but the family is already a kind of community of its own, dependent for nourishment on the wider culture. Through the recent teachings of the church—if not actual practice in specific parishes—such nourishment is available. But the work of building a strong base still remains the work of mothers, fathers, children, and members of the extended family.

William James, the American philosopher, had a saying which Dorothy Day frequently repeated, about the practicality of modest beginnings and actions. "I am done with great things and big things and great institutions and big successes, and I am for those tiny invisible molecular moral forces that work from individual to individual, creeping through the crannies of the world like so many rootlets, or like the capillary oozing water, yet which, if you give them time, will bend the hardest monuments of man's pride."

Family activity around peace and justice is that kind of "small capillary action," like the rivulets of nourishment in the earth. It is also one of the hopeful signs of the attentiveness of Catholics to social justice.

FAMILIES FOR TAX RESISTANCE

"The money required to provide adequate food, water, education, health, and housing for everyone in the world has been estimated at $17 billion a year," said the *Erie*

But What Can One Family Do?

Christian Witness. "It is a huge sum of money," it continued, "about as much as the world spends on arms every two weeks." And each family supports that spending in its annual payments, on April 15, to the Pentagon's tax collector, the Internal Revenue Service.

Although the extravagant military spending is almost incomprehensible, the effects of the overall policy are not. A family sees those effects in the faces of the poor and hungry in this country and around the globe. Confronted with such obvious injustice, individual families and communities, with support and cooperation from several bishops, have begun to take greater risks in resisting war taxes. They are making connections between their involuntary contributions to armaments and their obligation based on religious principle to disobey the law.

"I asked myself," one seminary student said, "would Jesus buy a nuclear bomb?" A suburban woman made the association between conscientious objection to the draft and conscientious objection to war taxes. "Because I couldn't be drafted, I thought there was nothing more I could do—then I realized that my money was being drafted for war." These people understand that the payment of taxes to the United States Treasury contributes to a possible nuclear holocaust.

Families face the same dilemma, as two young parents with four dependents, ranging in age from 3½ to 92, suggested in a recent letter about tax resistance: "We've prayed and fasted but as yet see no way that is within our grasp, and yet we know we can't just 'go along' much longer. We see our money harming people the world over. What should we do?" They are trying to choose between not paying the military portion of their income tax, living below the income tax line, or moving to another country.

Tax resistance is a serious matter, and anyone who decides to take this action should have adequate information and knowledge of the consequences, just as one should have sufficient knowledge of the consequences of paying those taxes (available from War Tax Resistance/War Resisters League). Stories and testimony by tax resisters and sources for community support give a sense not only of the value of tax resistance but also of the risks.

Since 1970, my family has refused to pay a portion of our taxes. The initial consequences were a seizure of our savings and bank accounts. In 13 years of marriage, we had managed to stash away the remarkable sum of $5.97. Since then, the IRS has been just as threatening, if somewhat less random: They simply take whatever amount they want out of my monthly paycheck.

My wife and I do not kid ourselves that this method of tax refusal seriously threatens the IRS's alliance with the Pentagon. But we are at least saying "No!" to that alliance; we are doing more than just voting against it. We are also voluntarily associating ourselves with those subjected involuntarily to the harassment by the state and with others who choose to resist in other ways. We need to do more.

For our children, tax resistance is complex and occasionally confusing. But it has made our conversations about peace and justice concrete. If they don't quite understand or agree with our practice, they do seem to get the message that we are serious about our criticisms of militarism, materialism, and capitalism. This does not mean that they have quit complaining about our old car, used furniture, and hand-me-down clothes. And I haven't either.

I wish that people supporting huge increases in the military budget for the 1980s asked two questions raised by all parents about any family expenditures: "Does it make sense? Can we afford it?" The answer to both questions would, I think, be "No" from a justice perspective. The results of such budgeting by the federal government is war, not peace, and suffering, not aid, for the poor. Such legislation by the United States Congress increases the global armed forces of this country beyond anything since World War II. It will cost at least $1.5 trillion by 1986, seriously threatening the economy and further fixing our already warlike stance before the world.

Each year, also, military spending creates fewer jobs, according to data from the Department of Defense, the Congressional Budget Office, and the Bureau of Labor Statistics. John Olver, a Massachusetts state senator, said, in supporting a resolution calling for a bilateral nuclear weapons freeze, that while $1 billion spent on the Pentagon employed 45,000 people, that same billion dollars for civilian use would employ 73,000 police, 76,000 teachers, or 85,000 nurses. Senator George McGovern's argument supported him: "Almost any private or public alternative will yield more jobs per dollar than arms production." Military spending is not only immoral; it is also a waste of money.

Edmund Wilson, one of America's major men of letters, wrote that although income tax has occasionally been imposed as a means of relieving the poor, "the really serious impositions have been due to the commitments of Washington to civil or foreign wars or to convictions of the imminence of a foreign one." That description of the relationship between war and taxes is still accurate. And Wilson's protest in the tradition of that colonial rallying cry against the British is still applicable: "No taxation without representation." The more families who join in saying,

"They ain't gonna pay for war no more," the greater likelihood there is of gaining back their country.

Ammon Hennacy, the Catholic worker and one-man revolution in America, justified his own war tax resistance in this way: "In rendering to Caesar what is Caesar's and to God the things that are God's, most people stick up for Caesar. It's time somebody stuck up for God."

THE PARISH

For many Catholics, the first—and at times the most difficult—extension of concern for peace and justice beyond the family is the local parish. In this work, parents still face the same opposition that many people faced in that first burst of enthusiasm following the publication of *Pacem in Terris* and *Mater et Magistra.* Just because your family is ready to commit itself to social justice does not mean that local clergy and laity are ready to join in. And "readiness is all," as Shakespeare wrote in *King Lear.*

A midnight call from my brother-in-law in the Midwest dramatized the conflict that can arise as a result of raised consciousness. He had returned from an area meeting of the Physicians for Social Responsibility, a medical group organizing against nuclear war and armaments, terribly shaken by what he had seen and heard, in films and in talks—particularly by Dr. Helen Caldicott—during a weekend conference. "The situation is hopeless," he said; and given the predictions of nuclear war by the year 2000, it is difficult to think otherwise. He had been alerted to the threat of war in a way that few Americans are and will probably have to deal with the indifference of his fellow parishioners now that he is prepared to work.

Parents can understand his impatience very well. A mother or father deals with the same anxiety frequently in raising children, the conflict between knowing from experience what must be done yet knowing also that one cannot force children beyond a certain point. Coming on too strong may do nothing more than provoke them to adopt exactly the opposite point of view or simply to rebel.

I remember confronting a similar situation after returning from a conference on *Pacem in Terris,* sponsored by the Center for the Study of Democratic Institutions, just a year after that great encyclical was published. There I heard Paul Tillich, John Cogley, Marya Mannes, and a host of senators, scholars, and diplomats praising the wisdom and practicality of John XXIII's encyclical, only to discover that my fellow communicants in Indiana—and particularly those in area schools and churches—were not at all interested in its message.

Parents must not assume that simply because they are ready to bring good news of church teachings to the local parish that anyone, including one's own family, is interested in hearing it. The work is slow and often very discouraging; at the same time it is astonishing what a few people can do when they are patient, persistent, and competent. And frequently the people one least expects are not only willing but anxious to commit themselves to education and action.

In recent years an extensive array of educational materials on social justice has become available, from manuals and books in religious education, to bulletins and films for parish councils and directors. The difference is reflected in the religious education of our younger children, in contrast to that of the older ones. As interest in and commitment to justice deepens in the church, publishers are finally responding to the need for new materials, with books, films, and tapes telling the stories of Dom Helder Camara, Mother Teresa, Archbishop Oscar Romero, Dorothy Day. A parish peace and justice committee can be crucial in publicizing and circulating such materials.

In some dioceses, the office of Catholic Charities has provided draft counseling information. That agency, with links to Third World apostolates, as well as to the poor in the local community, dramatizes the relationship between hunger and justice locally and internationally. The office of urban ministry, with its commitment to the inner-city, can also provide the necessary social analysis on the effects of poverty in the parish and diocese.

The office of Catholic Charities in one diocese initiated a series of events dealing with hunger that included radio talks by members of a subcommittee on hunger of the coalition on peace and justice; a diocesan group for education and action; a series of letters to the editor of the local newspaper and a series of articles on a related theme by clergy and laity in the diocesan newspaper; a telephone tree by people who agreed to provide a monthly meal for the local Catholic Worker House of Hospitality and soup kitchen; and workshops on Bread for the World at area religious education congresses and educational association meetings.

This campaign eventually spilled over into the general community, making hunger and its causes significant concerns in the region. Practical approaches to feeding the hungry in the local community were publicized (with students in religious education regularly responsible for cooking and serving a meal at the Catholic Worker community, as a part of their "love in action" program). There were also theoretical discussions devoted to understanding the systemic causes of hunger in the world, with a corresponding effort to address them through the political process.

In the parish or diocese, people hear the perennial complaint: "If only we could get a lot of people involved, then something could be done about violence and hunger," or "If only the bishop or the mayor or the state representative joined us, then things would change." And, yes, it is true that altering the consciousness of people in positions of power can lead to altering the way society works. But it is also true that the only way to change the system is to change oneself. Which brings us back to the parish. Until people change one by one, they are not going to change by the thousands. Even the president or the bishop cannot alter people's priorities and the course of events unless those people are committed to do so at that time.

And the battle is never totally won. Once the network is established, "keep on keepin' on," as the poet Etheridge Knight says: Arrange for films on peace and justice at religious education classes and in parish halls; bring speakers, including members of missionary orders, for programs at the public library; write regularly to the local and diocesan newspapers about antiwar demonstrations and legislation that is crucial to the movement; incorporate peace principles through hymns, readings, poems, and stories, as well as by accounts of those on the front lines in the nonviolent struggle for justice. And best of all: Schedule debates by people representing conflicting points of view on social justice. One of the best discussions on the draft I ever heard took place one evening in a small parish in Rockland County, N.Y. It came about as a result of a New Year's Eve homily by a parish priest, in which he described conscientious objection to military service as an acceptable choice for young Catholics. The immediate response was a storm of protest by those who supported the draft, war, and a huge military budget. They called a special meeting with the pastor, asking that the other priest be disciplined for even addressing such a topic during Mass.

But the ruckus raised by these pro-draft parishioners provoked a response in return from people in the parish who strongly supported what the homilist had said. Several of their sons had been conscientious objectors during the Vietnam War and others recently took the same stance. At the subsequent meeting, a member of the parish council acted as coordinator during an address by the pastor and moderated a lively debate among men and women of all ages and persuasions. It was a remarkable— and I must say rather inspiring —occasion, seeing that many people talking about such basic moral issues with a seriousness that is uncommon in contemporary American life.

Both sides—those supporting conscientious objection and those opposing it—presented their positions well. The pastor came prepared also, reading and citing basic church teachings by popes and American bishops that supported the right to conscientious objection. The other priest was not only right in raising the issue, he said, but also informed in the moral and theological position he espoused.

A similar result was achieved—though, again, not without debate—in my own parish, when Tom Cornell, cofounder of the Catholic Peace Fellowship and former editor of the *Catholic Worker*, conducted a day-long workshop on "Catholics and the Draft." The Catholic Peace

Fellowship, founded in 1964, regularly provides materials and speakers for workshops and discussions of this type and deserves to be better known among parents and teachers in parishes, schools, colleges, and Newman Centers.

As early as 1968, in *Human Life in Our Day*, the American hierarchy recommended approval of selective conscientious objection for those refusing to serve in wars "which they consider unjust or in branches of the service (e.g., the strategic nuclear forces) which would subject them to performance of actions contrary to deeply held moral convictions about indiscriminate killing." This document, a proper subject for various parish programs, raises basic questions about the traditional just war theory and supports those who would selectively disobey laws or commands contrary to Catholic teaching.

Since Vatican II, education through the parish and parochial schools on peace and justice has improved considerably. There still is a long way to go. In a changing church, that work must be done by laity who sometimes are better informed, better prepared, and more knowledgeable, in regard to the family, particularly, on how to proceed. The old complaint about priests and bishops not doing anything is seldom relevant; often enough, it is simply not true. Or, more appropriately, it is a complaint that can be made equally against clergy and laity.

The United States Catholic bishops, for example, and several recent popes have done the basic teaching at least. All parents need to do is to read them—*Renewing the Earth: Catholic Documents on Peace, Justice, and Liberation,* edited by David O'Brien and Thomas Shannon is a useful, inexpensive guide—to see how faithful the hierarchy has been in calling Catholic social teachings to attention.

A recent statement by Bernard Flanagan, Bishop of Worcester, calling for the beginning of the process of disarmament, "unilaterally if necessary," is representative. "The basic issue is not 'national security'; it is the more fundamental matter of defending human values and the survival and future welfare of the whole human race," Flanagan wrote. "Pray for peace! Write our leaders and urge an end to the nuclear arms race! Demand the reduction and eventual elimination of all nuclear weapons. . . . America must set the example; the alternative is final destruction."

What is needed now is a well-defined program of giving flesh to those words, through peace and justice centers throughout the United States and through action programs established by Pax Christi, the Catholic Peace Fellowship, the U.S.C.C. office of peace and justice, and several dioceses.

To repeat, even as few as two, three, or four people in a parish, if they are competent, persistent, and cooperative, can accomplish a great deal locally and regionally. For that reason, several other models for education and action in the following pages may appeal to individuals and families. In each case I have tried to keep the three criteria mentioned by Father Henri Nouwen in mind: prayer, resistance (saying "No" to death, and "Yes" to life), and community.

THE SCHOOLS

I hesitate to recommend activities for parishes and schools or make suggestions for increasing family awareness if I have not actually tried them myself, for fear of sounding hollow. And I must admit, as Carol Bly does in her wise, witty, and practical book, *Letters from the Country,* that "I am an expert at ducking out of political work." Having come clean, I can now mention a few useful activities that worked in educating my family and me, if not in changing the course of history.

Elsewhere I have talked about the importance of the way the past is presented through history and biography. Family members need to know of other models that might sustain them when they decide how they want to live. If, as David Dellinger has said, the best history is written by people who struggle against war, oppression, and hypocrisy, then parents must know these histories and teach them to their children. In such books, as Dellinger adds, the reader sees people's struggles "to incorporate into their own lives and organizations the values that led them to oppose [social] evils in the first place."

This attempt by families to learn about their past in order to build on it came to mind in a recent conversation with a black teacher from the South, the mother of three children. She told me of her concern that her own children understood little about the significance of the civil-rights movement in that region, even in her hometown of Little Rock, Ark. where some of the major confrontations took place. In school, they heard little about George Washington Carver, W.E.B. Dubois, or lesser known people who labored to end racism and injustice long before the civil-rights movement took place. The woman and I talked about how hard it is to keep "people's history" alive, particularly since publications for young people concentrate almost exclusively on today's events, without reference to the past, even the recent past.

The matter is further complicated by the fact that

textbooks emphasize "big campaigns" or actions of the rich and mighty, neglecting or ignoring the modest beginnings of movements for social change, such as the women's movement in the 1850s, workers' struggles around 1880, or draft resistance in 1918. It is not that books and films about these modest origins of nonviolent campaigns are unavailable; they are just not pushed commercially at educational conventions and, therefore, quickly drift out of fashion.

Peace-education programs in some public and parochial schools are working, however, in various parts of the country, to keep that "people's history" alive. The programs recommend alternative models from the past and describe the kind of world young people want to live in by the year 2000.

Each year in Dade County, Fla., for example, the schools conduct a contest to which children submit poems and posters on the theme "Reaching out for Peace"; in Nashville, Tenn. there is a program on "Creative Response to Conflict" in the schools; and the city council in Cambridge, Mass. told the Civil Defense Department to prepare a publication saying "why no step short of nuclear disarmament by all nations could protect Cambridge against nuclear war." The council did so after condemning the department's evacuation plan for the Boston/Cambridge area as useless. Following that debate, the city of Cambridge initiated a peace education program in the schools. (Information on similar programs elsewhere can be obtained from The Children's Creative Response to Conflict Program, Fellowship of Reconciliation).

In the Cambridge project, small children are encouraged to make lists of things that all people need (clean water, a safe home, sunshine, food, love). They learn songs, dances, and myths of other cultures to acquire a sense of the similarities and differences between themselves and their contemporaries in other lands. They talk about the values of cooperation over competitiveness, during games that can be "won" through shared effort.

Children who watch television are encouraged to discuss their favorite programs, to identify those that are violent or sexist, and to tell how and why. They discuss how these programs define men and women, boys and girls, and whether people of different races and cultures are presented honestly and accurately in most settings.

High-school students, on the other hand, look closely at the comparative cost of a helicopter and a school, a bomber and a hospital, an aircraft carrier and new housing for a whole section of the city. Students in our area wear a T-shirt with this slogan printed on it: "It will be a great day when our schools get all the money they need and the Air Force has to hold a bake sale to buy a bomber." Young people are sometimes more aware of the economics of the arms race than parents think, and questions about comparative costs are often the subject of class speeches, debates, and compositions.

One of the best writing assignments I discovered for young people asked them to list values important to them, such as love, friendship, family, success, justice, competition; to rank the values in order of their preference, and then to indicate why their first five choices were important to them. It was a difficult assignment, for many of them had never been asked those questions before by an adult. I suggested that they write to an adult audience, indicating how they thought their values agree with their parents' or were in conflict with them.

The values discussed in these assignments are appropriate in various classes: in writing, speech, history, literature, and biology, as well as politics and religion. I have suggested the rationale and implications of only a few. Additional examples are available in the publications of Pax Christi and the National Council of Churches as well as the Unitarian Universalist and Congregational churches.

Teachers are especially wise to invite to their classrooms and assembly programs activists who are thoughtful and persistent in staking their lives on what they believe. When the students meet people who embody peace and justice principles in their own lives, it helps revive their interest and recommits them to their support.

Students and young people need to know about such people, to learn about alternative ways of working, of being professionals, and of living as Christians. Frequently, a person in the local community is even better than a media star or an "expert from the next county." A local architect, for example, who combines resistance to nuclear armaments and power with an alternative energy program in his own home has educated many people in our community to the advantages of solar energy.

At no time is the need for adult models greater than during adolescence. At that very moment, because of their rebellion against their parents, young people look for different styles of being an adult, their mother and father being almost powerless to influence them directly. It is then that peers, teachers, and adults can effectively strengthen the values of the family (or undermine them). Young boys and girls try out various points of view, through arguments and attitudes that they pick up in school, on the street corner, or through the media. Likely as not, these viewpoints will be in conflict with whatever the parents stand for.

At such times, parents find it difficult to be patient or to adopt an attitude of "wait and see." And at that point, also, young people often find their religious faith inadequate to the pressure that they feel outside the home. There is no more conformist or tyrannical culture than teenage culture, not only in the U.S. but also in much of Western Europe, and many people simply take on the shabbier values of American society that define human beings primarily as consumers.

In 1976, the administrative board of the American bishops expressed a particular concern about another source of education in the schools, the media, and their obligation to be "truly responsive to the public interest." This obligation is sometimes better met by diocesan media than it is by the popular media, with their commercial orientation and reliance upon major networks. Some dioceses produce films on social justice, such as the excellent documentary, *Excuse Me, America,* produced by the Archdiocese of San Francisco, about Dom Helder Camara's visit to this country and his comparison of poverty here and in Latin America.

Another film useful in peace education is *Lovejoy's Nuclear War,* a 60-minute prize-winning documentary about a young man's victory over the nuclear power industry. On a cold, clear February night in 1974, Sam Lovejoy, the principal subject, toppled a 500-foot weather tower near his home on the Massachusetts-Vermont border. His civil disobedience was an effort to stop the construction of a multimillion-dollar nuclear plant on the Connecticut River.

In the film, viewers see and hear the testimony of Lovejoy's neighbors, including the local constable who arrested him, the members of the jury who eventually tried him, and the public relations director of the utility company that opposed him. Prosecuted for "willful and malicious destruction of personal property," he was eventually acquitted when the townspeople recognized that his action probably prevented the pollution of the river and contamination of animal, vegetable, and mineral life on the Montague plain and river valley.

I recommend this film particularly because it is a positive, even inspiring account of a historical incident. More important, it shows what one person, with the cooperation of his fellow human beings, can do to make the world a better place. By his simple, but courageous, act, Sam Lovejoy made a difference. Another significant point about the film is that Lovejoy took dramatic action only after trying many other means to alert the townspeople to resist the power company. He had made several legislative appeals, over a period of time, but without success. I like the film also because it dramatizes the fact that ordinary people, if given the appropriate facts, occasionally make humane decisions and that thoughtful resistance to abusive power, once in a while, achieves positive results.

The film illustrates the relationship between Lovejoy's struggle and previous struggles against injustice in American history, with testimony by Howard Zinn, a historian from Boston University. The story implies that alternatives to the status quo exist beyond the ones imposed on us by industry or entrenched power. Ideal for classes, for discussion groups in the home and peace and justice centers, or for parish programs, it is one of many available through Green Mountain Post Films, and similar filmmakers and distributors.

PEACE AND JUSTICE CENTERS

One of the most sustaining organizations in keeping a family's or community's attention focused on peace and justice is a local, regional, or diocesan center. Such a center provides tapes, books, discussion groups, and places for meetings, as well as other resources for education and action.

The style and emphasis in these centers vary from diocese to diocese and in different areas of the country, depending upon the priorities of the region. This is as it should be, since each area of the country faces particular problems at different times. In Connecticut, a state where roughly 80 percent of workers' income is derived from war manufacturers, Electric Boat, United Technologies, and so on, peace and justice centers devote much of their attention to the military budget, protesting against nuclear submarines and Trident missiles. In Minnesota and South Dakota, the emphasis in recent years has been on the Native American movement and the defilement of the landscape by land-based missiles and the Air Force. In Oklahoma, particularly as a result of the case of Karen Silkwood, an employee of a nuclear plant who died mysteriously, the peace movement has focused upon the dangers of nuclear waste and plutonium deposits. In Texas and California, the justice movement emphasizes the rights of Mexican Americans and the United Farm Workers.

As George Wald has said, all people working for peace and justice are united, even though each person stitches the garment at a different point in order to repair the tattered fabric.

Of the various peace and justice centers throughout the country, three might serve as models to others: the Centers for Reflective Action, in Holyoke and Worcester, Mass. and the Pax Center, in Erie, Pa. These centers provide resources for family education and action, as part of a Catholic response to the signs of the times. They are one of the significant recent developments in American Catholicism, following a pattern set by the Quakers and the American Friends Service Committee to meet similar needs after World War I.

At the present time, the American Friends Service Committee, with headquarters in Philadelphia, has ten regional offices throughout the United States. Quakers carry out programs through them for individuals and families, endeavoring to make the centers themselves models of justice in action. In addition to the permanent regional offices, in Dayton, Ohio, High Point, N.C., San Francisco, Calif., and seven other locations, there are also family summer camps, combining relaxation and education. The Avon Conference, held in New Hampshire, Vermont, or in Maine each July, provides thoughtful and sustaining programs for parents and children, covering a wide range of social issues. AFSC was also the first peace organization in my experience that made child care a part of its efforts for social change, adding another dimension of justice to its impressive organization.

Through the Centers for Reflective Action, the Pax Center, the Thomas Merton Center in Pittsburgh, and several diocesan peace and justice centers, Catholics have begun to develop new models that illustrate how faith and justice are joined.

The Center for Reflective Action, Holyoke, Mass. founded in 1976 by the Sisters of St. Joseph, provides a place for meditation and study, as well as a contact point in western Massachusetts for meeting and discussion. There parents and teachers find books, slide presentations, tapes, study guides, and games for use in the home or school. There is a room for prayer and quiet reflection or for people needing time to think. The center also gathers volunteers for work in the nearby Springfield, Mass. soup kitchen, which provides meals for street people. Out of this center there developed a network of residents who took in Puerto Rican families temporarily during a rash of arson attacks on the local Spanish-speaking community.

Next door to the center, several mobile homes provide shelter for migrant families who come annually to work in the fields at harvest time. The center is, in other words, a place where the many issues of peace and justice are visible and immediate and where families can think about their own lives in relation to the issues. It is an ecumenical center, with materials that link various religious traditions and encourage interfaith cooperation on special projects, and it houses the regional office of the New England Catholic Peace Fellowship, founded in 1971. Since its opening it has been a model for other women's religious communities throughout New England who have since developed other centers along similar lines.

In central Massachusetts, the Center for Reflective

Action—known locally as the Worcester Connection—provides some of the same services for a large urban community. It is located in an inner-city building which includes Abby's House, named after the great abolitionist Abigail Kelley Foster, a temporary shelter for battered and homeless women. The Worcester Connection, funded originally by several religious congregations of women, has increasing support from laity. The present directors are members of the Sisters of St. Anne and the Sisters of St. Joseph, with additional support from the Sisters of Providence, Sisters of Mercy, Sisters of the Assumption, Sisters of the Presentation of the Blessed Virgin Mary, Sisters of the Holy Union, as well as Xaverian and Medical Missionary Sisters.

The center provides offices for the regional *Clergy and Laity Concerned Newsletter* staff, a retreat space for women with books and places for study on women's issues, a small chapel, and living quarters for those working in the inner-city. In less than a year, the Worcester Connection has substantially increased not only the visibility of peace and justice work in the diocese, but also the work of clergy and laity in programs among the various congregations and parishes.

The Pax Center in Erie, Pa. is housed in the former quarters of the Oblates of St. Benedict and has educational resources including a shop selling items for children and adults produced by workers around the world. A library of books and audiovisual materials, and local offices for Pax Christi serve a wide community beyond the confines of the local parish. The residents of the center include eight Benedictine sisters, two priests, several laity, and two sisters from other religious congregations. This community of people also does much of the work for Emmaus House, a soup kitchen several blocks away, serving one meal a day to people who have no other place to go.

The Pax Center resembles, in many ways, an agronomic university in a style that Peter Maurin suggested, where the worker becomes a scholar and the scholar becomes a worker. It is a combined House of Hospitality and Continuing Education Center that daily performs the spiritual and corporal works of mercy.

LEGISLATIVE ACTION

Children grow up with only vague ideas about how laws are enacted, perhaps because discussions about it in most schools remain abstract. In the family, parents can make the workings of government clearer by initiating discussions of the issues, particularly as children reach the teenage years. Children can develop a sense of how society works or doesn't work, in specific instances, by meeting political figures and studying their careers.

At times, the most time-consuming, frustrating, and seemingly futile kind of work for social change is dealing with state and national legislatures. Yet it is in the halls of senators and representatives that some proposals for long-term social change will be debated and brought to significant states of development. Passing a law obviously does not bring peace and justice into being, but it can further both of them. "Voting for the right," Thoreau said in *Civil Disobedience,* "is not necessarily doing anything for the right"; but it does encourage others who are doing the work.

Voting something into law also establishes in the public

mind and in history that some peace and justice principles won the agreement of most people. For that reason, work for changes in the law is productive. And before that, lobbying for or against particular issues contributes to the education of voters and legislators alike.

One woman in my town has had a significant effect on educating local legislators on peace and justice issues, such as capital punishment, selective service, the draft, and military spending. By her letters to the local newspaper, visits to congressional representatives, and faithful phone calls in support of peace and justice, she has won not only the agreement, but also the respect of elected officials. During the Vietnam War, she was better informed on the selective service laws than any but a few people in Washington and was known to correct several mistaken rulings against local registrants. Her ability to point out discrepancies between the law and the actual administration of Selective Service undoubtedly contributed to the draft's being put on stand-by status in 1973. Similar citizen action might help to re-establish congressional control over other national policies, especially where the Pentagon runs the show.

Through her persistent, careful, and timely information on changes in the law, this one woman educated the local community, from young and ignorant journalists writing articles for the newspaper to experienced and often ignorant attorneys, about how to give advice to draft registrants. Once when she and I went to testify on behalf of draft appeal before the Senate Armed Services Committee in Washington, I found that her letters and phone calls had not gone unnoticed by the legislators who found time to speak with her about important legislation even when they didn't follow her advice.

My point in mentioning this "majority of one" lobby for peace—a woman with three children, two of whom are conscientious objectors—is to emphasize the importance of letters and congressional visitations. With the help of the Friends Committee on National Legislation, which publishes a newsletter on coming votes, as well as up-to-date voting records for all legislators, people can raise the level of public discussion and sometimes influence a vote.

Letters to representatives and senators must also insist on replies. In some instances, the reply will be a standard one written by a staff member. But the lobbying effort should not stop there. Send a response to that letter, pointing out how you agree or disagree, where the argument falls down or is based upon inaccurate information. Find out when the representative will visit your area and arrange to meet, accompanied by others from your community who share your views. Most people may be surprised to find that their representative is often less well-informed on an issue than they are—another reason that visitations and letters are important.

Letters to legislators should be brief, informed, and to the point. Do not preach. State the position, give supporting evidence, and encourage the representative or reader to join. Sometimes it is useful to include addresses or places where additional information or assistance is available. When writing to the newspaper, remember that the letters try to convince all the readers, not just the editors. Below is a sample letter, urging people to stop the nuclear arms race; it received, in slightly different form, favorable responses from readers.

TO THE EDITOR:
The administration's arguments justifying the development of the neutron bomb are like statements out of a

terrible nightmare. Hearing them, anyone may be reminded of similar arguments by Hitler's generals during World War II.

The consequence of those policies was devastation and death for millions of people. Isn't that what we are preparing for ourselves and our children in building neutron bombs?

In a recent *New York Times* review, Kai Erikson, a professor at Yale University, asked, "What kind of mood does a fundamentally decent people have to be in . . . before it is willing to annihilate . . . a quarter of a million people for the sake of making a point?" Clearly the Secretary of Defense is in that mood in deciding to produce the neutron bomb.

I am not sure what anyone can do to dramatize the insanity of our country's warlike policies at the present time. But people committed to a different course of action may wish to know about the Catholic bishops' statement in 1968 condemning the neutron bomb and about *Peacework*, 2161 Massachusetts Avenue, Cambridge, Massachusetts 02140

These publications, at the very least, remind readers that not everyone has lost his or her ability to distinguish between a moral and an immoral society. They encourage us to remain human in the midst of a very dehumanized and dehumanizing administration.

NAME

ADDRESS

Children should be encouraged to make their opinions known as well. They can give valuable support to a sympathetic legislator by volunteering to canvass, address letters, and do similar services. Working as an aide provides excellent training in presenting a person's opinions on public issues, a skill that will be useful in later life. Such involvement will suggest to young people how hard people work in public life and how dependent they are on an informed citizenry.

DIRECT ACTION

Any decision to resist injustice, in word or deed, may rightly be described as *direct action*. This discussion, however, is limited to leafleting, picketing, and civil disobedience. The first two kinds of direct action may involve all members of the family; the last one is probably limited to parents. But in any social-justice action, it is good to be informed on all three and their contributions to social change throughout American history.

Public demonstrations that support or protest public policies can be effective in changing these policies. In recent history, the United Farm Workers through the use of boycotts and protests have enabled previously unorganized laborers to achieve better salaries and working conditions. That effort has led to credit unions, community educational programs, and a whole range of physical and spiritual benefits for previously deprived people. Some migrants, with the assistance of individuals and families throughout the country, have finally achieved social justice in the face of powerful opposition, not only from agribusiness and large growers, but also from organized labor, which originally withheld support.

The struggle by the farm workers' union to protect the rights of workers not covered by the labor legislation of the 1930s alerted many middle-class people to the injustices of the system. Their struggle is similar to that of other laborers around the world, in the face of multinational corporations and agribusinesses.

116

The main object of picketing and leafleting is the correction of a wrong, but they also accomplish many smaller effects. And every member of the family can play a part in them. They include making an issue public that has been ignored by the press, the opposition, and the general populace; correcting misinformation broadcast by the media and those in power; and reminding customers that their economic power can be used for justice. Many people have a latent sympathy for workers, the people who make up most of the world's population, and are hesitant to cross a picket line or to ignore a leaflet that appeals for just wages and practices.

Writing and passing out leaflets apply to public events, primarily, but they are appropriate for discussion and action in the family, as well. Writing a good leaflet, one that is clear, precise, and interesting, is not easy. Here are some questions a leaflet writer should ask: Is the leaflet clear? Are the arguments convincing? Was the first impulse to read the handout or to drop it in the nearest wastebasket? Was it interesting graphically? Was the issue important, and why?

I remember asking Sidney Lens, peace activist and author of some 20 volumes, how he learned to write books. A veteran of labor struggles, he looked at me as if I weren't very smart and answered, "By writing leaflets, of course."

Preparations must also be made before picketing. To be effective, any demonstration must be nonviolent in attitude, word, and action. A demonstration is an effort to win people to peace and justice, not to impress them with size and numbers or to intimidate them. In such a gathering, it is important to have well-informed and articulate persons to speak to the press and to answer questions by passersby in a courteous but firm manner and to deal with hecklers in the same way.

In all demonstrations at a public place, it is usually advisable to alert the local police, so that they will not be caught by surprise and therefore more likely to be violent in a response to unpredictable events. The local police can be the demonstrators' allies, particularly if the demonstrators are long-term residents of the area and if the police know that the demonstrators are serious and trustworthy about their purpose and tactics.

The presence of children at a demonstration, as opposed to a silent vigil, is a problem. It's best not to take them unless they express a definite interest. Parents should never take advantage of their power position. Consciences are best formed by free choice, not by coercion. The parents make clear what their values are, teach them as effectively as possible, live them, and then hope for the best. And patience with children, as with social change, is a revolutionary virtue.

The decision to commit civil disobedience, a riskier form of direct action, is not easy and should not be treated lightly. Gandhi, the great apostle of nonviolent resistance, was the first of many people to speak at length about the preparations to be made before entering into it. Even when a particular law is a bad one, it is a serious matter to break it. It is serious because most people have a deep respect for the law. It is one of the human endeavors, as St. Thomas More maintained, that helps to make public discourse and action more orderly and, on occasion, more civilized. It has protected people against the rule of tyrants.

But the law can also provide a cover for unscrupulous

people to do despicable things, such as gathering wealth and power at the expense of the poor and workers of the world. Or as Ammon Hennacy, the great war resister and Catholic Worker, used to say, "A bad law is no better than any other bad thing." Such harsh truths are not easily conveyed to children, and parents are wise not to dwell on such confusing and even disorienting aspects of modern culture. Nonetheless, it is also important to try to convey to young people the reasonableness of those who break the law for conscience's sake. Meeting people who have committed civil disobedience or seeing them interviewed on television, as well as reading and discussing their statements in the home, helps to clarify complex questions surrounding them.

Social change often requires extraordinary measures, as the great liberators of the past learned during the time of the American Revolution, the abolitionist, labor, feminist, and civil-rights movements. In each case, change came about only when people were willing to sacrifice themselves for a better world. This included going to jail, not out of some wish to be dramatic, but simply because taking a stand for justice brought them into conflict with those protecting the status quo. People in power had the courts, the police, and the Army to back them up, and in many cases, in the United States and abroad, they still do.

In the early part of the 20th century, many advocates for workers' rights and just wages unexpectedly found themselves in jail because of their efforts to make life better for most people. In 1912, two workers named Joseph Ettor and Arturo Giovannitti, for example, went to jail on false charges, because they spoke for non-English-speaking workers in the mills and factories of Lawrence and Lowell,

Mass. Mothers and fathers who were involved in that struggle, known as the strike for Bread and Roses, emphasized the immediate effects of bad working conditions on family life by sending their children to New York City, so they would be out of danger. Through such efforts many families now enjoy better standards of living, with social security benefits and paid vacations. These stories are often fascinating to children, as part of their own history, and deserve a place in the education of young people for peace and justice.

Other men and women have broken the law for conscience's sake in the struggles by workers in the sit-down strikes in Michigan in the 1930s and in the more recent armaments protests in Seattle, Omaha, Amarillo, Groton, Conn., and Seabrook, N.H. The successful witness and influence of Jonah House and the Community for Creative Nonviolence, in demonstrations at the Pentagon and the White House, is a testimony to the effectiveness of civil disobedience in exposing injustice. Many families, including young children, join them in that effort, particularly on special feast days, such as the feast of the Holy Innocents, just after Christmas, and during Holy Week.

Such matters are appropriate for serious discussion, meditation, and prayer among families, even those not prepared to risk breaking the law in their pursuit of peace and justice, but willing perhaps to support or assist others who do. Philip Berrigan and Elizabeth McAlister have said that, as parents of small children, they feel particularly compelled to take those risks, as a testimony to their hope in the future and to a world for their children. Molly Rush, who joined seven other members of the Plowshares 8 to dismantle a nuclear missile in Pennsylvania, has six children; yet she and her husband also decided they must address the threat of nuclear war as a family, enduring the sacrifices that her jail term imposes. Theirs is a hard choice, not easily entered into and certainly never without the understanding and support of others involved.

There are precedents, however, in many other areas of life. Military families, as Elizabeth McAlister has said, make continual sacrifices in order for fathers to go away to war. Is it not even more appropriate for parents and children to make equal sacrifices in order to wage peace at home?

A movement informed by Catholic social teachings is dependent upon the work of many people, with each person making a basic contribution in the family and the wider community. And that movement will not take place unless people change their ways. Each day, thousands of people in industry, government, universities, and even the church are paid large salaries to continue policies leading directly to injustice, repression, and nuclear war. Many others tolerate systems that make starvation and repression almost inevitable for our brothers and sisters at home and abroad.

Commitment to peace and justice means doing something to bring them about. It may be necessary first of all to face feelings of powerlessness and anger and then to imagine a better integrated society. What would it be like to live in a world not burdened by a huge arms budget and by political barriers to the production and distribution of food for hungry people? What can my family and I do to address even one aspect of these injustices locally or internationally?

The means employed to correct these problems are as

important as the goals we establish. "There is no peace," A. J. Muste argued, "peace is the way." Similarly, in the words of Martin Luther King, Jr., "The choice today is no longer between violence and nonviolence. It is either nonviolence or nonexistence."

Parents must accept people, their own children or other adults, where they are. "Assume that they are doing the best they can to break out of their feelings of powerlessness," as Frances Crowe, a veteran peaceworker, says. "Project your most hopeful moods, but accept others' feelings of powerlessness and share your sense of it, too."

Try to understand the facts behind hunger and violence, but remember a person doesn't have to be an expert, just someone committed to the truth and to the alleviation of needless suffering and death. Action based upon these principles will not only deepen a person's commitment; it will also encourage others.

There are many options, when it comes to actions as a family or as an individual, Frances Crowe concludes, "from active resistance to licking stamps to leafleting to assisting with child care at an event. All peaceful actions are important in the creation and maintenance of the movement for a peaceful world."

6

Teach Your Children Well

"You who are on the road
Must have a code
That you can live by."

Graham Nash

The popular song by Crosby, Stills, Nash, and Young, "Teach Your Children Well," gives the right advice, even if it has few recommendations about how to go about it. Here I want to indicate where parents can look for sustenance and support to maintain themselves and to educate their children over the long haul. Under the best circumstances, religious education and renewal move along with each stage of development, a process that continues to the end of life. So parents are rightfully concerned about their own as well as their children's education for social justice. Or as Crosby, Stills, Nash, and Young put it in the second stanza, "Teach your parents well."

One of the principal challenges faced by any person concerned about peace and justice is to keep informed about events and issues. This is not always easily done. In spite of the fact that the popular press is relatively free of direct control by the state, it is nonetheless influenced by those in power, by people who want to further their own interests.

In many cities and towns (my own is an example) the people who own the local newspaper (as well as the radio or television station, a defense-related industry, or other

123

major enterprises) are not likely to advocate fundamental social change for the benefit of everyone. As with owners of most profitable businesses, these people have probably never read the encyclicals of John XXIII, Paul VI, or John Paul II and would hardly approve of them if they did. It is common to read editorials in the daily newspaper that dismiss the values and programs recommended in the encyclicals as utopian, or worse, as Marxist, even if the proponents are some of the most respected and admired members of the Christian community.

Almost any person who proposes social changes in favor of the poor and oppressed is in danger of being called Marxist in the mistaken notion that only Marx and his followers have that kind of concern. But as Robert J. Carleton, M.M. has said in his response to those who attacked Maryknoll missioners in Latin America, a Christian committed to social justice "knows that one system of government—whether it be Marxist or a corrupt military or civilian government—can be just as oppressive as another." The parents' task, not unlike the missioners', is to form their own consciences as well as others', to remember that as children of God they have rights, and to confront any person or government which denies those rights.

Many journalists and television broadcasters also complicate matters by treating any reasonably literate press release from politicians, popular entertainers, or wealthy industrialists as reliable news. It is not always a conspiracy by the few who dominate the world so much as a reluctance of the many to speak directly and frankly about injustices before their eyes. Yet the teachings of the church and recent popes are quite clear about the need to see things as they are for the poor and the victims, rather than as those in power wish us to view them. It is necessary "to *call by name*," John Paul II said, every social injustice, discrimination, and violence inflicted on the body, the spirit, the conscience, or the convictions of members of the human family.

It is not an easy task to dig for the truth, and espousing unpopular opinions about what must be done for justice's sake seldom leads to *success* as the word is defined by contemporary culture. Journalists, announcers, and media experts who double as entertainers or public relations consultants to the courts of influence, however, are generously rewarded, and their power over the popular imagination is staggering.

The confusion and obfuscation of much political writing is traceable to the efforts of those who use language to disguise rather than to reveal the truth. That is another reason people must work hard to find out what is going on. George Orwell, in his important essay "Politics and the English Language," said that much political language "is designed to make lies sound truthful and murder respectable, and to give an appearance of solidity to pure wind." What Orwell wrote in 1946 is even truer today.

Part of parents' work of keeping informed about peace and justice is to become attentive to language, so that they recognize and expect some clear image of themselves and of other human beings in what they hear and read. Such skills go back to basic ways parents communicate with their children, how they speak to them and listen to them, and what kind of expectations they give children about language and truth. There is a saying that "If an idea cannot be expressed in language understandable to a reasonably

attentive seventh-grader, someone's jiving someone else."
Parents must listen to what they are saying to their children, not simply for the child's sake, but for their own
understanding of what is being heard.

This holds true for religious ideas as well, including
those related to social justice. That is why I devote considerable attention later in the book to what publications parents have around the home and why an emphasis on reading, writing, listening, and speaking is essential to the quest
for peace and justice. Parents need to show children what
can be gained from knowing about people and experiences different from their own. Reading is important, for
example, "not merely as a skill," as Bruno Bettelheim says,
"but as a means of gathering valuable information—of ac-
quiring meaning."

What Bettelheim learned through his own close observa-
tions of children is important to what I am saying here
about keeping informed and about what parents make
available to children as they are growing up. "It is not
enough that the parents read," as Bettelheim says. If they
don't enjoy reading and say what is gained from it, children may not learn from it.

Nor should parents worry too much about exposing
children to reading that is anxiety-producing, Bettelheim
adds. Fairy tales do that by dramatizing symbolically many
of the stresses about love and hate, sexuality and death
which children face in their daily lives. It is better to relate
a serious story about the Puritans and Thanksgiving than a
sentimental one, for example. Such a story might tell about
how the Dutch couldn't stand the Puritans and kicked
them out and "about how undesirable rigidity can be and
the need for tolerance." Through stories about struggles

for justice, complete with a happy ending, children learn that people in history have something to say to them.

PUBLICATIONS

In some areas of the United States, the local diocesan newspaper, through its contacts with religious news services in countries around the world, provides more international news than the local secular newspaper. The quality and range of diocesan newspapers vary greatly, however. Just how much information on peace and justice gets printed depends upon the level of consciousness among local clergy and laity and the professional standards of the editor. But there are several models to point to, including the *Church World* (Maine), *Catholic Free Press* (Worcester, Mass.), and *Sooner Catholic* (Oklahoma City). The *Catholic Free Press*, for example, publishes all major documents related to Catholic social teachings as they appear, with commentary, and articles related to local issues. Recently, in response to the diocesan Coalition on Peace and Justice, the newspaper carried a series of articles by area clergy and laity on what they are doing to address the issue of hunger. Contributors included a local religion teacher in a Catholic high school, a member of the Catholic Worker community, a Sister of St. Joseph who founded a home for battered and homeless women, and the director of the Catholic Charities office. Such approaches made a global issue concrete and visible on the local level.

Few developments in journalism in the past two decades are more dramatic and consequential than the steadily improved standards in the publications of the American church, as it became a bit more self-critical and less parochial in its concerns. Much of the credit for this change must go to the *National Catholic Reporter,* still one of the best sources of information on Catholic social teachings in this country and abroad. Edited by lay people, but governed by a board of clergy and laity, it has been instrumental in educating a generation of Catholics to the teachings of the Second Vatican Council and beyond, focusing attention on abuses of justice inside as well as outside the institution.

There is also "the world's greatest newspaper," the *Catholic Worker,* dedicated since 1933 to building a new society within the shell of the old, one in which, as Peter Maurin said, "it is easier for men and women to be good." Even those people who do not follow its anarchist and pacifist philosophy find the *Worker* both a beautiful as well as a reliable guide to basic information on the central issues of the time. Its dedication to investigative reporting, its contacts with persons deeply engaged in resisting injustices on a variety of fronts gives it an authority that few publications possess.

Over the past two decades I have often read about an important event related to civil rights, human rights, or war resistance in Asia, Africa, Latin America, or the United States, or have been alerted to a consequential writer or thinker for the first time in the *Catholic Worker.* Ignazio Silone, author of *Bread and Wine* (1937), one of the great religious novels of this century, Thomas Merton, and Alexander Solzhenitsyn are but a few of the authors who appeared in its pages long before they were taken up by the popular press.

Another amazing thing about the *Catholic Worker* is that its old issues are as useful and informative as the daily newspaper, for the social concerns first addressed by the *Worker* in 1933 still exist—poverty, hunger, racism, militarism. Its writers, because of their commitment and persistence in the face of these issues, speak with real authority about the causes of injustice and how people can work to bring about change.

A few years ago, when someone complimented Milton Mayer, contributing editor to the *Progressive* magazine— another valuable, independent monthly, devoted to social justice—on the strengths of his magazine, he said, "Well, we keep trying to be as good as the *Catholic Worker* and maybe someday we'll make it." Milton Mayer was obviously being modest about his own publication, but I think he was also suggesting the standard by which he measured any publication's commitment to human values.

Another inexpensive and valuable source of information, especially useful for families, is *Maryknoll*, a monthly magazine published by the Maryknoll order about its missions in countries around the world. Handsomely illustrated in color, it gives brief, but informed commentary by clergy and laity who daily give their lives feeding the hungry, curing the sick, and doing other corporal and spiritual works of mercy.

Each issue of *Maryknoll*, organized around a particular theme, draws attention to a particular message of the Gospel, indicating where it applies to a concrete issue. The issue of May 1981, for example, focused on "Challenges to Workers and Church," with quotations from John XXIII's *Mater et Magistra*, Paul VI's *Populorum Progressio*, the poems of John Paul II, photographs of factory and farm workers from Bolivia, Tanzania, Malaysia, as well as brief illustrated biographies of two great friends of the working class, Dorothy Day and Mother Jones. The magazine makes an effort to suggest the commonality of people in this country and abroad and the interrelatedness of the secular and the sacred, the corporal and spiritual natures of humankind.

For children as well as parents, the articles in *Maryknoll* are both timely and useful—brief, but well-written. Parents pressed into service at the last moment by children with reports due the following morning in history, geography, or civics classes will be especially grateful for the attractive photographs. One of my friends, an anthropologist, whose interest is not primarily religious, regards this magazine as a valuable and reliable source of information on other cultures. A teacher's guide for religious education or other classes is available with bulk orders of the magazine, and the Peace and Justice Office, at the same address, provides an excellent *News Notes* on recent events, speakers, resources, and materials.

Salt is another monthly magazine that helps parents learn about social justice. *Salt* encourages individuals and families to do what they can in their day-to-day living to bring about a more just society by showing what others have done within their own world. *Salt* also offers articles which give both sides of various social issues, allowing readers to make up their own minds about their stands on the issues.

In addition to these publications, there are the excellent journals of opinion, some available on pamphlet racks at the back of the parish churches or through subscription. A family cannot, for financial reasons, subscribe to them all, but parents can make an effort to see that they are available at the local library, in the school library, or at the regional or diocesan peace and justice center. Almost any issue of *Commonweal, America, U.S. Catholic,* and *New Catholic World* includes articles addressed to specific events reflecting the church's commitment to social justice. The same is true of the outstanding ecumenical magazines, such as *Christian Century, Christianity and Crisis,* and *Sojourners.* These publications are all, in different ways, more independent than standard journals of opinion, which are sometimes owned by a principal stockholder and thus less likely to harbor "unpopular" causes than they did in the past. Among several well-known monthlies or weeklies, however, the *Progressive* and *Nation* are persistently independent, even courageous, in their commitment to human rights.

In addition to the articles in these magazines and newspapers, a few of them offer special services for education and action. The *National Catholic Reporter,* for example, produces tapes and cassettes, with study guides for particular issues; and it regularly lists courses and institutes on peace and justice, including family programs, in various areas of the United States, with visiting lecturers, scholars, clergy, and laity.

It is not easy to stay informed, and parents need to seek out local and regional guides as well. In this instance the newsletters provided by the American Friends Service Committee, through its ten regional offices, are invaluable. *Peace Work,* published by the AFSC, is one extraordinary example of such a service. Other sources are available through the diocesan urban ministry or peace and justice commissions. National organizations, such as the Office of International Justice and Peace of the United States Catholic Conference, Catholic Peace Fellowship, and Pax Christi are other principal contacts for newsletters.

One family, obviously, cannot read them all. That is why

families depend so much on a community of people, each person reading different publications that have been found trustworthy over a period of years. An attentive reader will come to realize that there are some writers and editors whose commitment is to the welfare of everyone, not just of a few. These journalists are not engaged in strengthening the hand of those already in power or increasing the profits of multinational corporations. They know that such powerful people and organizations are fully represented already in the daily newspapers, in expensive advertisements on television, and—openly or behind the scenes—among lobbyists in state and national legislatures.

TELEVISION

The unrepresented, like the poor, are always with us. But as Michael Harrington pointed out in *The Other America* they are often invisible. As concerned citizens, parents have to find them and their advocates in newspapers and magazines not always on the newsstands at the mall, on Main Street, or in the local drug stores. Beginning with World War II, there has been a steady rise of America's fortune as a world power, coinciding with a centralization of propaganda: the dependence of the public for news on a few major networks, a decreasing number of newspapers, and a few independent magazines and journals of opinion.

This condition places a burden on parents, with limited leisure time and a growing family, to find alternative newspapers, independent media, and news services. Yet in each section of the country there are contemporary ver-

sions of *I. F. Stone's Weekly,* that vigorous insistent voice of
sanity from 1958 to 1971. Written, edited, and distributed
by I. F. Stone and his wife, it published more real news in
four 8½ × 11 pages than most publications ten times its
size. A prize-winning film, "I. F. Stone's Weekly," tells how
they did it and reminds the audience of the journalist's
responsibility to set public matters in an historical context
and to point out the implications of public policies. Stone,
now regarded as a hero, used his energy and intelligence
to dig for the truth, and there are several younger journalists, publications, and filmmakers who maintain his
high standards of reporting at the present time.

Television is an important means of informing young
people and adults on public issues, with occasional outstanding programs or films about peace and justice. Some
examples are the excellent "Bill Moyers' Journal," "Dorothy
Day: Still a Rebel"; the biographies of Martin Luther King,
Jr., and Jane Pittman; occasional interviews with public
figures—the Phil Donahue session on the Plowshares 8,
with Molly Rush and Daniel and Philip Berrigan; or
documentaries on hunger in America and the Third
World. Often these programs are later available on film
through regional library systems. But these authoritative
and insightful presentations of the human condition are
not the ones most immediately available to children.

The opinion of a reasonably objective judge of children's programs is pertinent here. Writing in the *Family
Factbook,* a standard reference on health, housing, work,
income, and the American family, Donald J. Cohen and
Ada S. Branzegee state that only one or two national television programs for children show adults as respectful of
their rights and feelings or present them with positive

models. "Too much TV aimed at children shows violence and disrespect, condones hitting, beating, and murder, and portrays the tough, brutal, and insensitive person as someone to be admired." In most commercials, television's message to children is clear, that "deception is a widely practiced way of trying to achieve a goal." So, also, one might add, are violence and injustice.

These conflicting messages were obviously picked up elsewhere by children before television. I make a point of mentioning what Cohen and Branzegee call "the new educator of community standards" merely to recognize its contribution to people's acceptance of violence in the wider culture and its popularity as another complicating factor in the moral education of children.

I am not advocating that parents not allow their children to watch television. Barring them from it may only make television seem more desirable than it is. I am suggesting, however, that parents encourage children to think about what they see and to be aware of the value systems inherent in the medium and the message. Showing children how much more interesting reading is than watching television may lead them to ignore what is bad on the screen and to watch what is good. Programs that dramatize the conflicts and sufferings of real people obviously can contribute to their education for peace and justice as well.

THE CONTEXT

To keep informed is to see events in context, that is, to maintain perspective in the midst of many conflicting opinions and answers. Gore Vidal is fond of saying that Americans never remember anything that happened before last Tuesday, and this loss of memory or destruction of memory is often the cause of our failure to stay on track, to keep our heads straight in the midst of conflicting truths.

Until recently American Catholics had maintained a strong commitment to their own interests as working-class people. Their voting record since 1928 was consistently liberal, supporting a worker's right to organize, benefits for the poor and unemployed, educational loans, and benefits for the lower-middle class.

Conflict over these interests within the Catholic community is inevitable and will probably increase. The affluence of American Catholics, particularly, has led to increasing conservatism, even reactionary politics, among Catholic college graduates. The strong bond between social justice and the Catholic population needs to be re-established, and the Catholic social teachings in the writings of the popes and of American bishops are an important means of doing that. They are a reminder of the best in that history, as well as a challenge to parents to recommit themselves and their children to social justice. That will not happen without some thoughtful work in home, parish, and community by people who are informed, persistent, and nonexclusionary in their approach.

Such work is confused by the fact that sometimes even the closest associates, those people who are personally good, kind, and generous, seem very distant from social-justice theory on a universal scale. They are people who would be the first to bring food to a family that was hungry or give away their last dollar to a person who was broke. In the local parish they are the first to volunteer to visit the elderly or the sick or to open their homes to visitors from abroad. But they are sometimes the same people who make racist remarks about blacks or Puerto Ricans, who justify sexist language, and who support the production of nuclear bombs or submarines.

The same people who would sacrifice a great deal to feed hungry children in Guatemala vote for legislators or a president who support policies victimizing the people of Central America. These parishioners would never knowingly hurt another human being, yet they agree with their government's repeatedly sending military aid to El Salvador, the Philippines, or Argentina, to be used against their brothers and sisters in those countries. How can families encourage them to make the necessary links and to understand the contradictions?

7

Liturgies

"What a fellowship, what a joy divine,
Leaning on the Everlasting Arm;
What a blessedness, what a peace is mine,
Leaning on the Everlasting Arm."

Traditional Hymn

The Catholic Church in the modern world is, among
other things, a great depository of learning, with links to
the history, art, and religious traditions of many ages and
countries. In spite of its limitations, the church remains
one of the few institutions that tries to uphold the essential
sacredness of life. Through its teachings it insists upon the
precious value of the individual soul—the value of "the
valueless"; and through its liturgy it provides sustenance
and inspiration by celebrating those principles.

I was reminded of this recently during a homily by a
priest whose sermons often wander aimlessly about the
readings for the day. Biblical texts with an obvious peace
or justice theme prompt him to some vague or trite reflection on "God's love" or some similarly overworked theme.
But on this Sunday, beginning with the rather unpromis-
ing subject of the royal wedding, he moved on to the importance of liturgy in our lives as a means of asserting the
dignity and mystery of human life.

The homilist went on to point out that feeding hungry
people, whoever they are, is required by justice. Referring
to the Sunday Gospel, the story of the loaves and fishes, he

made a wise comparison between Christ's generosity toward the crowd and the American government's policy in the distribution of food to starving people around the world. Jesus, the priest added, did not ask people what political party they belonged to before he fed them. He did not pass from one person to the next to say, "Be my disciple and I'll give you something to eat." He fed the people because they were hungry, not because they agreed or disagreed with him—and undoubtedly his enemies were among the crowd.

After the homily, the congregation, with full organ accompaniment, sang the majestic 19th-century hymn by Frederick Faber, "There's a wildness in God's mercy/Like the wildness of the sea;/There's a kindness in his justice/That is more than liberty." Someone had obviously given a lot of thought to the liturgy for that Sunday, and as a consequence the comments by the congregation after Mass were spirited and thoughtful.

I chose to write about this liturgy not only because of its message, on a justice theme, but also because of the reminder it contains of the potential power of the church as a guide and inspiration. Perhaps families can maintain a commitment to social justice without remembering its theological depth, but they need not be forced into that position. Through the liturgy, parents have a means not only of strengthening their own commitment but also of celebrating that commitment with their children and the wider community. Through the readings, hymns, and ritual, they can say, "Here is a community we wish you to grow into, one that celebrates the essential mysteries of life and death, peace and justice, in word, music, and gesture. Here you will find strength, reinforced through the Eucharist, even if we are not around."

Through liturgy parents teach social justice, relying on the power of religious symbolism to instruct and enrich their lives; they make use of the various arts—music, painting, and dance—as the church, in its wisdom, has done for centuries. Through liturgy children get a feeling for values associated with peace and justice and celebrate them in a widening circle of relationships outside the immediate family.

Nothing helps sustain a commitment to peace and justice more than a liturgical life directed toward that end. The corporal and spiritual elements of work for social justice are so interrelated that they cannot be separated from one another without affecting, perhaps weakening, both. A difficulty arises, however, from the fact that few clergy, laity, communities, or parishes, have managed to fully integrate the two elements. Since liturgical reform and a renewed emphasis upon social justice took place at about the same time, it is understandable that much work still needs to be done to make both of them integral to church life.

If liturgy, properly understood, is the public service of the clergy and the work of the people—the word derives from both of these roots—then the liturgy of Christian families devoted to peace and justice should reflect these facts. That is done through readings, music, and movement, including meditations on the biblical roots of nonviolence, prayers for victims of wars and injustice, and celebrations on the anniversaries of people and events associated with social justice.

Liturgy is, first of all, an art. It has form as well as content, and if the form is ill-defined, ugly, or trite, then the message is likely to be the same. It is therefore not easy to develop liturgies that carry the message of the Gospels and reflect the concerns of the congregation, whatever the theme.

A good liturgy, as the liturgist and theologian George Garrelts says, helps to carry a person through the week—the problem being, as he also noted, that most liturgies seldom get a person past Tuesday. For liturgy to be central to the lives of religious people, it must have the marks of good art, including integrity and simplicity. And unless it reflects the central place of peace and justice in the life of the congregation, people are unlikely to find the necessary spiritual sustenance to maintain those values in their own lives.

In time, as people begin to see a closer connection between their own lives and religious celebration in simple, unstilted, nonsexist language, liturgies will probably improve. In the meantime families must do what they can to encourage better styles of celebration in their parishes or to initiate their own. They must contribute to the development of vigorous liturgies that make Catholic social teachings central to the symbolic life of the church. Some have done so, in Newman centers—especially in the Midwest and Southwest—in inner-city parishes, ecumenical groups, or resistance communities.

Part of the task of educating self and others is to gather appropriate readings and hymns that draw out the implications of those justice and peace themes in the Old and New Testament. And I have a few suggestions about how to do that, after one negative and representative example.

One Saturday afternoon, after a day-long conference of talks, workshops, and a demonstration on behalf of the United Farm Workers at a nearby supermarket, some 200 Christians gathered in a large hall for worship. The liturgy had been conceived as the concluding event of a marvelous day—informative, interesting, even inspiring, because of the way in which committed people shared their hopes and fears, failures and successes of the past year.

The day-long event was the annual meeting of the regional Catholic Peace Fellowship, on the theme of disarmament, and the response of people provided the sense of renewal and reawakening that continued work on these issues requires.

But what happened when the group came together for worship? Almost nothing, in the way of music, language, or celebration. Judging by the Mass, the feeling was that these people had never even heard of a "new awareness" spoken of in the papal encyclicals—that they were there to bury the church rather than to give it new life and meaning: In their motley of 1950s vestments the six or eight concelebrants looked like a group out of an old Cecil B. DeMille film lot; the music, unsingable, of course, with one soloist concertizing in a voice that no one could hear and songs that no one ever heard of; the readers mumbling through the Gospel and epistle, and so on.

How is it, with the richness of the Gospels, the variety of music, ancient and modern, full of character and beauty, and all that talent and courage and intelligence in that group of men, women, and children, that everything fell flat? How is it that on such occasions Christians settle for lifeless, ignorant, and uninspiring celebrations?

I am not advocating what I heard at a Sunday Mass on another occasion—a congregation that was almost drowned by the perpetual sound of a high-school choir and orchestra, of electronic music and songs by Neil Diamond and from *Jesus Christ, Superstar*. Silence and contemplation are as important to liturgy as sound and gesture. And there are great hymns out of the Protestant and Catholic traditions, where people in the past spoke of their hunger for justice in noble language and music.

Contemporary readings, for private prayer and meditation as well as for public liturgies, also help to focus religious celebration on justice. Among the best recent writings are the essays of Thomas Merton, Dorothy Day, Father Henri Nouwen, and Father Daniel Berrigan. *Cry Justice: The Bible on Hunger and Poverty,* edited by Ronald J. Sider, "a Bread for the World Reader," includes selections that are suitable for short prayers before meals or liturgies conducted by the family at home or on public occasions.

Several contemporary poets have also written works that dramatize the emergence of the sacred in everyday life, including liturgies that follow traditional parts of the Mass. A particularly beautiful one, from which the following brief selection is taken, is Denise Levertov's *Mass for the Day of St. Thomas Didymus* (copyright by Denise Levertov, 1981):

GLORIA

Praise the wet snow
    falling early.
Praise the shadow
    my neighbor's chimney casts on the tile roof
even this gray October day that should, they say,
have been golden.
                    Praise
the invisible sun burning beyond
    the white cold sky, giving us
light and the chimney's shadow.

Praise
god or the gods, the unknown,
that which imagined us, which stays
our hand,
our murderous hand,
             and gives us
still,
in the shadow of death,
       our daily life,
       and the dream still
of goodwill, of peace on earth.
And gives us
the sun,
the weather,
flow and change, night and
the pulse of day.

For children's liturgies, there are the powerful, simple,
and artful parables of Jesus, dramatizing elemental struggles between good and evil, that young people find particularly fascinating. All the dark forces that make up
much of their own inner life at that age are personified in
the folk-like tales of the Old and New Testament: the pro-
digal son, the ungrateful servant, the good Samaritan. In
the writings of Isaiah and Jeremiah, one hears about God's
punishment for those who refuse to care for the poor, the
widowed, and the elderly. Liturgies built around these
themes, in language and songs appropriate to children,
provide a basic introduction to the dominant themes in
recent Catholic social teaching.

Whether or not liturgies work, however, depends upon
the people who make them, that is, everyone in the congregation. The celebrant is obviously the key, as director,

mediator, or choreographer, shaping and holding things together. The celebrant is not, however, a superstar; nor should there be other stars involved who set up barriers between themselves and the congregation. That is one reason that concelebration with several ministers is a mistake. It is not only bad theology; it is also bad drama. In such situations, a pack of priests or ministers say, in body language, "Some people at this gathering are more equal than others, *and don't you forget it!*" The celebrant functions best not by being dramatic, but by allowing everyone to speak through him.

These principles hold true for all religious celebrations. Realists will recognize, also, as Virginia Sloyan and Gabe Huck do, in *Children's Liturgies,* that young people regard liturgy with mixed feelings. It is primarily an adult activity. There are, nonetheless, ways to make children feel less excluded than they might be and to encourage their participating whenever they are willing to do so.

Besides family prayer, religious feasts can be celebrated in the home in a number of ways. Occasional Masses, with young children participating in scenes associated with Gospel stories, as at Christmas or Easter, are useful introductions to the central mysteries of faith. A re-enactment of the Seder feast, on Holy Thursday, has been an annual celebration by several families close to us. Although the children grumbled about attending five years ago, now, in adolescence, they participate willingly in the readings. The older ones have even been heard to say they looked forward to the event. A special feast in the late spring or summer, such as Pentecost, with a liturgy centering around a family or community picnic, enables parents to assign roles to children—carrying banners or reading statements by contemporary activists for peace and justice—that they find tolerable, even during their more rebellious years.

Our approach to these matters has been not to force the issue or to have any great expectations about our children's participation in formal liturgies. I am not at all sure that this is the best way to proceed, but at this point I am reduced to thinking that we did the best we could with six small children. If I had the chance to re-do the very early years, I might stress their becoming involved as altar boys and altar girls and perhaps as members of a church choir. These activities along with participation in the offertory procession can provide an excellent introduction into the history of religious celebration. Singing hymns to the accompaniment of a guitar in a small group gives children a feeling for good music, but there is no substitute for the glories of a mighty organ, with harp, trumpet, and drums on major feast days, or for the beauties of church music from the Middle Ages and the Renaissance.

On a more modest scale, religious celebrations involving children (aside from major feasts, where tradition provides a number of activities) should focus on birthdays of famous people, anniversaries in the family or community, and public holidays. For the purpose of illustration, I can point to readings, songs, and hymns that might be used on anniversaries of Martin Luther King, Jr. (January 15 or April 4), letting these examples suggest the general approach that might be adapted to a variety of settings.

Photographs or films or tapes of King's speech ending the March on Washington might introduce the theme for the day, with an opening hymn, "Amazing Grace," "We Shall Overcome," or even more traditional music that applies to the justice motif. Readings from the book of Exodus and St. Luke's description of Jesus proclaiming liberty to captives are appropriate for the first part of the celebration. A homily or meditation based upon King's "Letter from Birmingham Jail" or his reflections on non-violence, which are filled with biblical language and symbolism, lead naturally into dialogue among the congregation, including struggles or stories of discrimination from their own lives. During and after the distribution of the Holy Eucharist, symbolizing, among other things, the sacrifice of activists in all liberation movements, hymns such as "Once to Every People and Nation" and "The Lord of the Dance" provide an appropriate conclusion.

The life of Martin Luther King, Jr. is only one of many lives that provide suitable subjects and themes. The regular church calendar includes the feasts of the Holy Innocents, Catherine of Siena, Thomas More, as well as more recent members of the faithful, such as Dietrich Bonhoeffer or the Maryknoll missionaries who died in El Salvador for justice and peace.

Even a rather traditional Mass can center on these concerns and include similar activities. I remember, for example, a moving and stately liturgical dance during an offertory procession at a conference on peace and justice. The musical accompaniment and poem, "Bread and Roses," about a famous strike in Lawrence, Mass. in 1912 were especially appropriate for an event sponsored by a women's congregation.

Although most Catholics will undoubtedly work through the traditional structure (and building from within is preferable, if the atmosphere and leadership are not totally oppressive), here are two models for developing nonterritorial parishes around peace and justice issues.

The first is the Floating Parish of Worcester, which originated in 1968 and lasted for a decade.

A brochure that served as both an introduction and an invitation to that parish outlined the reasons for starting a group that was both interfaith and intercommunion. Initially ordained clergy from major denominations and then laity as well served as principal conveners. In working to build a community that gave form to its spiritual values, The Floating Parish acknowledged that it was trying "to discover a contemporary idiom for religious celebration" and that that effort was "a natural extension of people's work together in antipoverty, civil-rights, and peace activities."

The Floating Parish chose texts and themes that gave liturgical expression to that work with weekly collections "offered to those people (such as the Catholic Worker, Southern Christian Leadership Conference, and Emmaus in Peru), working in this country and abroad to alleviate people's suffering." It followed this pattern for a decade, and its introductory leaflet provides some concrete ideas about alternative liturgical communities organized around social issues.

Another parish with similar emphasis, but structured differently, is the Community of the Living Spirit, Waukesha, Wis. Organized in 1971 it has maintained a nonterritorial parish, with an ambitious educational program for adults and children and numerous activities expressing social and political concerns. Over a ten-year period, the community, which meets in the gymnasium of a local school, has found various ways, some traditional, some new, to carry out the general goals listed in Article II of the community's by-laws: (1) to be more aware of the needs of people within and outside the community, and to minister to them; (2) to encourage personal growth through education, "in understanding God's will for the members, collectively and individually"; (3) to celebrate life through expressive liturgy, with emphasis upon "the fundamental goodness of the life Jesus Christ has proclaimed to us"; (4) to remain open to change; and (5) to sustain and encourage one another in carrying out these goals.

There is obviously no one way to develop peace and justice liturgies that is more effective or more appropriate than another. Even the most traditional forms, done with an artful integration of music, readings, and a homily—by people for whom these concerns are more than Sunday morning preoccupations—can give spiritual strength and renewed dedication. But close attention needs to be given to Catholic social teachings since Vatican II, with this useful guidance by Placid Murray, O.S.B.: "To speak of liturgy as evolving is not to assume that the liturgies of the past were wrong and must now be corrected. Indeed, the creation of liturgical form suitable to the needs of our age carries with it the implication that in this world of change the liturgy must continually be renewed so that it can be relevant to the human situation and to people's understanding of the reality of God."

An emphasis upon social justice, which has been an essential part of the teaching of Christianity from the beginning, is a natural encouragement toward the revitalization of what recent theologians have called "the alienated liturgy." In new liturgical beginnings—in traditional parishes or in communities such as The Floating Parish and the Community of the Living Spirit—there are signs of new forms growing out of the lives of people committed to peace and justice.

As a participant in such liturgies I have been struck many times by the power inherent in the words of the Gospel, in the music of traditional hymns, and in the symbolism of bread and wine. I have been reminded also of the inspiration that brought these older practices into being. Many of the religious rites at the center of the Judeo-Christian tradition came out of the plight of oppressed people—in the desert, on pilgrimage, in the catacombs, in persecution. Reenacted in a church, on the picket line, or on sites of oppression and violence being reclaimed for justice and peace, these rites reveal anew the depths and nature of this tradition.

In this sense liturgy serves an aesthetic and educational as well as religious function in the church. And these questions might help parents and children develop suitable celebrations: Can the liturgy be planned and integrated in such a way as to impress upon the celebrant and congregation the significance and majesty of religious truth? Can it reflect the concerns, the pain, sorrow, and joy of all God's people, in a manner that will help them care for one another? Is the worship formulated in a gesture that is natural, graceful, and human?

That is what one looks for in creating liturgies that resonate with the rhythms and stories of the past and the issues of the present. Those are the ones that strengthen and sustain individuals and families as they journey toward social justice, celebrating some achievements along the road.

Parents have all been a part of such liturgies, at one time or another. It is essential to insist on that standard in their local parish or in liturgical communities in order to insure the spiritual growth of their children and, in a sense, their own sanity and commitment over the years.

Epilogue:
"Signals Across Vast Distances"

"Because there is one loaf of bread, all of us,
though many, are one body, for we all share the
same loaf."

Romans 12:17

The promotion of peace and justice, especially when it conflicts with contemporary culture, can be complicated, and neither families nor individuals are likely to maintain their commitment without the support of a wider community.

Parents are asked to proceed on faith when they educate their children in a new direction, toward new loyalties and new ways of living. A remarkable poem by Muriel Rukeyser, beginning, "I lived in the first century of world war," speaks to this point. She honors men and women of the past who set up "signals across vast distances,/considering a nameless way of living, of almost unimagined values." A courageous writer, who spoke and acted against war and injustice from the 1930s until her death in 1980, Rukeyser knew that living the values of social justice involved considerable risk. It means being honest, authentic, and persistent in envisioning a society in which no one is favored simply for being rich or powerful or white or male or female.

In the past, many people felt that the American church

neglected the welfare of the poor, the victims. It seemed overly concerned with personal salvation, to the exclusion of Christ's message in the Sermon on the Mount or the spiritual and corporal works of mercy. Such tasks were left to the women who nursed the sick or to the foreign missionaries in leper colonies. Likely as not it was the people who prided themselves on *not* being religious in the conventional sense—people such as Bertrand Russell or Simone de Beauvoir or Albert Camus—who addressed the issues of nuclear war, sexism, imperialism, and exploitation. They were the thoughtful voices in the 1940s and 1950s calling for peace and justice and for resistance to the state, to corporate capitalism, and to religious institutions.

By the 1960s, however, the call to peace and justice was strong in the writings of Catholic clergy and laity, including Thomas Merton and Michael Harrington, and the example of Dorothy Day, Ammon Hennacy, and the *Catholic Worker* was increasingly visible. It is important to remember that history as parents ground themselves and their children in the message of peace and justice.

For a parent, it is perhaps helpful to see Catholic social teachings as the church's attempt to re-establish priorities around the needs of human development. In some ways, the teachings simply recognize that the care and nurturing of human beings, the rightful task of any humane society, have been neglected by the wider culture and that the work of the Christian Church must make a central place for those values. The family, the first means of socialization, is the rightful place to learn and practice those skills. Such a transformation will involve a lot of work and necessary changes in the family structure, and now is the time to begin.

EPILOGUE

Over the past century, through the psychological studies of Freud and Jung as well as Piaget and Erikson, we have learned that basic human needs associated with growth in various stages of childhood and adulthood have not been satisfactorily met by our culture. The division of labor, for example, making child care the responsibility of women, has resulted in a complex and powerful limitation of men's experience, with a devaluing of skills essential to the welfare of all. The consequence has been a profound confusion about the values of life and meaningful work and an anxiety that can be very self-destructive. Is it any wonder that a society so alienated seems bent on nuclear suicide? And are we piling up neutron bombs and missiles because massive destruction is the only imaginable relief from the self-hatred that characterizes people's behavior toward one another? Finally, wouldn't it be more humane to restructure society, justly, rather than merely sing "I'm OK and you're OK" on the road to oblivion?

Beyond that, there is a strength and vitality in the church's teachings and a heroic testing of the boundaries of religious experience. It is a breaking open, in a sense, whereby the institution refuses to be bound by the imposed restrictions of Western culture and American capitalism. In such a movement, the church moves beyond an individualism and narcissism that narrows the message and teachings of Jesus and makes them subservient to middle-class morality.

The church teaches that a person cannot be prosperous, happy, and Christian at the expense of another person and that believing Christians are responsible for the welfare and development of their neighbors. This theme is obviously central to the Gospel, but through Vatican II and the social encyclicals, the church has focused attention on what had been reduced to a minor theme. Out of this new awakening come courageous acts by clergy and laity, such as one bishop's refusal to pay war taxes and another's act of reconciliation toward Iran, the nonviolent protests of the Atlantic, Pacific, and Great Lakes Life Communities, civil disobedience of the Benedictine Sisters for Peace, as well as a movement for a new social order.

In many ways, the church is discovering and exploring a new language, as a creative artist does in every age, seeking to understand and to describe the signs of the times. It is no simple task to find the language, symbols, and acts that best speak to a troubled world, and there may be mistakes. But there are precedents and people to look to for guidance. Recent American history provides models, as Muriel Rukeyser says in the poem, in "reconciling ourselves with each other, ourselves with ourselves," as we try "to reach the limits of ourselves, to reach beyond ourselves,/To let go the means, to wake."

In this book, I have tried to suggest how the family might contribute to that movement. I have recommended some models for imitation, readings for meditation, and possible actions. With the help of these writings, films, and community centers, and with liturgies for sustenance and inspiration, parents and children can not only participate in the work of peace and justice, they can also be a major factor in carrying that struggle to the church and to the world.

Resources

The following list of readings for parents and children (discussed throughout the book) is restricted to publications dealing with people prominent in American church history or in peace and justice issues. Those marked with an asterisk appeal to younger readers, who are particularly attracted to adventure stories and mythic tales.

Books

Anne Frank: The Diary of a Young Girl. New York: Pocket Books, 1952. The account of a group of Jews in hiding in Amsterdam during the Nazi invasion and World War II. Also a film and play.

*Louise Armstrong, *How to Turn War into Peace: A Child's Guide to Conflict Resolution.* New York: Harcourt Brace Jovanovich, 1979. An illustrated "Let Me Read Book" that is both witty and practical.

*William Armstrong, *Sounder.* New York: Harper & Row, 1972. A simple, but powerful rendering of black experience in the South, through the lives of a family and a dog; also an excellent film.

The Autobiography of Mother Jones, ed. Mary Field Parton. Chicago: Charles H. Kerr Publishing Co., 1974. A brief life of one of the heroines of early 20th-century labor struggles.

*Margaret Hope Bacon, *I Speak for My Slave Sister: The Life of Abigail Kelley Foster.* New York: Thomas Y. Crowell, 1974. A biography of a great 19th-century activist against slavery.

Daniel Berrigan, *Prison Poems.* New York: Viking Press, 1973; and *The Trial of the Catonsville Nine.* Boston: Beacon Press, 1972. Poems and a play based upon Father Berrigan's imprisonment for civil disobedience. The latter is also a film and on a record.

Philip Berrigan, *A Punishment for Peace*. New York: Macmillan, 1969. A selection of essays on the relationship between church and state, including the statement of the Catonsville 9, who burned draft files during the Indochina War.

Tom Blackburn, *Christian Business Ethics: Doing Good While Doing Well*, Chicago: Fides/Claretian, 1981. A clearly written discussion of the individual Christian's role in complex questions of business ethics.

James Breig, *Wave Good-bye to the Joneses: The Christian Use of Wealth*, Chicago: Fides/Claretian, 1981. A popularly written book about the claims of social justice upon an affluent society with practical guidelines for individuals to meet their obligations.

Dorothy Day, *The Long Loneliness*. New York: Image Books, 1958. The story of a great woman's conversion to Catholicism, and life as a writer, friend of the poor, and agitator for social change. See also her *Loaves and Fishes* (1963) and *On Pilgrimage: The Sixties* (1972).

*John Deedy, *Apologies, Good Friends: An Interim Biography of Daniel Berrigan, S.J.* Chicago: Fides/Claretian, 1981. A readable and intriguing account of a contemporary public figure.

*Marc Ellis, *A Year at the Catholic Worker*. New York: Paulist Press, 1978. A journal of a young worker's experience at St. Joseph House of Hospitality in New York City.

*Michael Garvey, *Confessions of a Catholic Worker*. Chicago: Thomas More, 1978. Reflections of a college-age student and worker at Peter Maurin House in Davenport, Iowa.

*John Howard Griffin, *Black Like Me*. New York: Signet Books, 1962. The courageous story of a white man who colored his skin in order to learn about racism and discrimination.

Hard Times: An Oral History of the Great Depression, ed. Studs Terkel. New York: Pocket Books, 1978. Interviews of people from the 1930s, including Dorothy Day, Cesar Chavez, John

Beecher, and many others involved in the worker's movement.

Michael Harrington, *The Other America: Poverty in the United States.* Baltimore: Penguin Books, 1962. An influential and readable commentary on the "invisible poor."

*Cecelia Johnson, *Her life for His friends: A Biography of Terry McHugh,* Chicago: Fides/Claretian, 1980. The story of the short and action-filled life of a young woman dedicated to discerning and serving the needs of others.

Martin Luther King, Jr., *Why We Can't Wait.* New York: Signet Books, 1964. A collection of essays, including "Letter from Birmingham Jail," a classic statement on peace and justice.

Denise Levertov, *The Sorrow Dance.* New York: New Directions, 1966. A selection of poems, especially "Life at War," by an outstanding author.

Isidro Lucas, *The Browning of America: The Hispanic Revolution in the American Church,* Chicago: Fides/Claretian, 1981. Traces the history, struggles, and aspirations of the Hispanics in the United States and points out the unique contribution they can make to their church and country.

Robert J. McClory, *Racism in America: From Milk and Honey to Ham and Eggs,* Chicago: Fides/Claretian, 1981. In a series of vignettes this book illustrates some of the typical effects of racism in the cities of this country and some of the work that is being done on the local level to combat these effects.

Thomas Merton, *The Nonviolent Alternative,* ed. Gordon Zahn. New York: Farrar, Straus & Giroux, 1980. Essays and meditations, including "Blessed are the Meek: Christian Roots of Nonviolence."

*George Orwell, *Animal Farm.* New York: Harcourt Brace Jovanovich, 1954. A classic tale of "how society works" at times.

Mary Bader Papa, *Christian Feminism: Completing the Subtotal Woman,* Chicago: Fides/Claretian, 1981. Graphically describes the pervasive effects of the sexism that is built into the institutions of church and society and suggests remedies.

Alan Paton, *Cry, the Beloved Country.* New York: Charles Scribner's Sons, 1961. The tragic effect of apartheid on two young men, one black and one white, in South Africa; later adapted as a play, *Lost in the Stars,* with music by Kurt Weill.

Chaim Potok, *The Chosen.* Greenwich, Conn.: Fawcett Publications, 1967. The story of two fathers and their sons, providing insight and understanding of Jewish tradition and heritage.

Henry David Thoreau, *Walden* and *Civil Disobedience.* New York: Signet, 1973. Reflections by "the majority of one" against injustice.

Gordon Zahn, *In Solitary Witness: The Life and Death of Franz Jagerstatter.* Collegeville, Minn.: Liturgical Press, 1980. The story of an Austrian Catholic who refused to fight in Hitler's war. Also a film, available from Pax Christi.

Organizations and Publications

The following list is by no means exhaustive. There are, in fact, many other organizations, publications, and resource centers that might be mentioned, including several listed in the text of this book. Among the valuable periodicals, in addition to those mentioned below, are *America, Commonweal, U.S. Catholic,* the *Progressive,* and *Sojourners,* whose addresses are available at most public libraries. All the organizations publish newsletters, as does the regional office of the American Friends Service Committee nearest you.

ORGANIZATIONS

American Friends Service
  Committee
1501 Cherry Street
Philadelphia, Pa. 19102
(215) 244-7000

Amnesty International
  (AIUSA)
308 West 58th Street
New York, N.Y. 10019
(212) 582-4440

Bread for the World
32 Union Square East
New York, N.Y. 10003
(212) 260-7000

Catholic Peace Fellowship
 (CPF)
339 Lafayette Street
New York, N.Y. 10012
(212) 674-8990

Center for Reflective Action
Mont Marie
Holyoke, Mass. 01040

Central Committee for
 Conscientious
 Objectors—An Agency for
 Military and Draft
 Counseling (CCCO)
2208 South Street
Philadelphia, Pa. 19146
(215) 545-4626

Clergy and Laity Concerned
 (CALC)
198 Broadway
New York, N.Y. 10038
(212) 964-6730

Community of the Living
 Spirit
Box 383
Waukesha, Wis. 53187

Eighth Day Center for Justice
22 East Van Buren
Chicago, Ill. 60605
(312) 427-4351

Fellowship of Reconciliation
Box 271
Nyack, N.Y. 10960
(914) 358-4601

Floating Parish of Worcester
41 Iroquois St.
Worcester, Mass. 01602

Friends Committee on
 National Legislation (FCNL)
245 Second Street, N.E.
Washington, D.C. 20002
(202) 547-6000

Jonah House
1933 Park Avenue
Baltimore, Md. 21217
(301) 669-6265

Office of International Justice
 and Peace, U.S.C.C.
1312 Massachusetts Ave., N.W.
Washington, D.C. 20005
(202) 654-6812

Pax Center
345 East 9th St.
Erie, Pa. 16503

Pax Christi U.S.A.
3000 North Mango Avenue
Chicago, Ill. 60634
(312) 637-2555

War Resisters League/War
Tax Resistance (WRL)
339 Lafayette Street
New York, N.Y. 10012
(212) 228-0450

Worcester Connection
21 Crown St.
Worcester, Mass. 01609
(617)756-1038

PERIODICALS

Catholic Worker
36 East First Street
New York, N.Y. 10002
Monthly; 25¢ a year

Maryknoll
Maryknoll, N.Y. 10545
Monthly; $1.00 a year

National Catholic Reporter
P.O. Box 281
Kansas City, Mo. 64141
Weekly $20.00 a year

Peacework
2161 Massachusetts Avenue
Cambridge, Mass. 02140
Monthly; $5.00 a year

Salt
221 West Madison
Chicago, Ill. 60606
Monthly: $10 for 10 issues

FILMS

Green Mountain Post Films
Box 229
Turners Falls, Mass. 01376
(413) 863-4754 or 863-8248

A Prayer for Peace

Based upon the conclusion of John XXIII's *Pacem in Terris*.

May God banish from our hearts whatever might endanger
peace.

May God transform us into witnesses of truth, justice, and love.

May God enlighten the rulers of nations, that they might
guarantee the gift of peace to all citizens, especially to those in
need.

May God enkindle our wills, so that we overcome the barriers
that divide us, cherish the bonds of mutual charity, and par-
don those who have done us wrong.

May all the peoples of the earth become as brothers and sisters to
one another;

And may that most longed for peace blossom forth and reign
among us always. Amen.